Kenneth Clark

S. M. U.

Christmas 1993

FALLIBLE
MAN

THE PHILOSOPHY OF THE WILL

FALLIBLE MAN

PAUL RICOEUR

Revised translation by
CHARLES A. KELBLEY

Introduction by
WALTER J. LOWE

New York
Fordham University Press
1986

Printed in the United States of America

CONTENTS

INTRODUCTION

WALTER J. LOWE
Emory University

PAUL RICOEUR was born in Valence, France in 1913. While study-
ing philosophy at the Sorbonne, he came under the influence of the
existentialist Gabriel Marcel. Interned in a German prisoner-of-war
camp during World War II, he studied the works of Edmund Husserl,
the founder of the phenomenological movement. Ricoeur's writings
range from his early explorations in philosophical anthropology, of
which *Fallible Man* is the premier example, through subsequent studies of the religious symbolism of evil, Freudian psychoanalysis, metaphor, narrative, and interpretation theory generally. Since 1970,
when he was appointed to the chair formerly held by Paul Tillich at
the University of Chicago, he has divided his time between responsi-
bilities in this country and in France.[1]

Rich in texture, expansive in scope, and indefatigably exploratory
in character, Ricoeur's is not a philosophy that lends itself to tidy
summary. Still it may be possible, by way of introduction, to retrace
something of the pathway along which his thought has moved: to
indicate a few of the most basic concerns and then to show how those
concerns, and the interaction between them, came to generate the
particular works which he did in fact write. As a means of interpreting the institutions and works of art which constitute our culture,
Ricoeur has often sought, in and through those various expressions,
an underlying human act, a generative "affirmation" of effort and desire. Without pressing the point unduly, we may ask to what extent
Ricoeur's own thought, and particularly his early work, may be interpreted in the light of such an originary affirmation.

This, then, is the question to be explored in the first section of the
present Introduction. The second section will focus specifically upon
the structure of *Fallible Man*, and the concluding section will seek to
reinsert the anthropology of *Fallible Man*, so interpreted, into the
larger context of Ricoeur's philosophy.

I

We find an instance of Ricoeur's orientation toward primary affirmation in an early essay in which he calls for a philosophical "humanism" which can provide a response to "the peril of the 'objectification' " of the human being. Humanism, understood as the struggle of thought against such objectification, extends beyond the common notion of the humanities: it becomes the effort to reclaim and reaffirm "the *élan* of humanity."[2]

In this light one may readily say that Ricoeur's own work is profoundly humanistic; in and through the interpretation of human experience, he has sought to fashion "a notion of being which is *act* rather than *form*, living affirmation, the power of existing and making exist."[3] But as Ricoeur's reference to struggle indicates, philosophical affirmation cannot remain simple and indiscriminate. Saying "yes" to the fullness of the human means pronouncing a resolute "no" to each of the various forms of reductionism, which would constrict or deny the reality of human freedom. The most obvious instance of such reductionism is the scientific positivist, the advocate of a narrow empiricism; but the reductionist label applies to any method which seeks to explain away the fullness of our experience by dismissing that experience as "nothing but" the effect of this or that underlying cause. Ricoeur's teacher, Gabriel Marcel, has posed the issue forcefully:

> We should have at this point to make a direct attack on general formulations of the type, "*This* is only *that* . . . *This* is nothing other than *that* . . .", and so on: every deprecatory reduction of this sort has its basis in resentment, that is to say, in passion, and at bottom it corresponds to a violent attack directed against a sort of integrity of the real. . . .[4]

The deprecatory spirit assumes many guises; there may be a behaviorist reductionism, a Freudian reductionism, a Marxist reductionism, a structuralist reductionism—and it is testimony to the robust character of Ricoeur's peculiar humanism that, at one point or another in his career, he has engaged each of these challenges in vigorous debate.[5]

But Ricoeur's way of approaching such debate tends to be more

irenic than Marcel's. Ricoeur is apt to suggest that the various forms
of reductionism are not so much wrong as one-sided. Like the blind
men who encountered an elephant, each is to be credited with having
laid hold of a part and having insisted upon its reality. The mistake
is in taking the part for the whole. In Marcel's language they have
fallen prey to the spirit of abstraction; in Whitehead's terms they have
succumbed to the fallacy of misplaced concreteness. It follows that
a truly humanistic philosophy, in contrast, must be unwaveringly
holistic; and indeed this too is an apt term for Ricoeur's thinking.
There is, in fact, no surer rule for the reading of Ricoeur than to
watch for the way in which he construes his chosen question in terms
of an apparent conflict between two contrasting aspects or poles—
and then proceeds to mediate between them: drawing the contrasting aspects together while yet preserving a certain productive tension or dialectic. One acute commentator has interpreted the entirety
of Ricoeur's work in terms of this dialectic of "kinship through
conflict."[6]

Such effort of thought is quite different from the bland assertion
that both parties to a dispute are somehow right. Ricoeur is clear
that "eclecticism is always the enemy of dialectic."[7] It follows, then,
that to accomplish a mediation of conflicting viewpoints the philosopher needs to have some anticipatory sense of the whole, some general notion of how the various isolated aspects fit together. And it
is at this juncture, in the effort to clarify the nature of the whole, that
we come upon what may be called "the humanist dilemma." For, on
the one hand, our first impulse may be to identify the two terms which
have thus far been central to our discussion—i.e., to say that the
whole of which we speak *is* in some sense the human. We may call it
human experience, perhaps, or human reason, or human potential.
And yet the moment we make this move, we are bound to sense its
absurdity. How obtusely self-centered, that we, the frail and transient
inhabitants of a minor planet in a minor galaxy, should take "the
human" to be the key to an understanding of reality!

But if, on the other hand, we are led by such chastening reflections clearly and emphatically to divorce our sense of the human
from our conceptions of the whole of reality, the consequences are
no less unsettling. For however we then proceed to understand the
whole—as the material universe, as the process of evolution, even as

some indeterminate spirituality—we are apt to find that the concreteness of human experience is all too readily swallowed up in an abstract and alien metaphysic. Indeed the grandest notions are precisely those which are most apt to be employed in ways that prove oppressive or manipulative. It is for this reason that one critic of modern culture has been driven to assert that "the whole is the false."[8]

Now I want to suggest that, for all of its complexity, Ricoeur's thought may be interpreted in terms of this humanist dilemma. Indeed, it may be argued that much of his richness and complexity actually *derives from* the struggle with the dilemma. Ricoeur's accomplishment, in this light, would be to have transformed the dilemma from occasion for despair, as in certain forms of existentialism, to occasion for constructive reflection; and to have enlisted the erstwhile reductionists as positive contributors to this larger struggle. By actively appropriating the dilemma, rather than ignoring or suppressing it, Ricoeur prepares the way—by his own distinctive, longer route—for what Marcel would call a meditation on the *mystery* of existence.

Thus, as we have seen, Ricoeur wants his thought to be rooted in the concreteness of human experience; everything must relate back, in one way or another, to human action. At the same time, as we shall increasingly come to see, he will not have a philosophy which is in any sense self-centered; he insists upon the strenuous discipline of continually *decentering* human (self-)consciousness. Accordingly his thinking becomes characteristically bi-focal, centering on human action *and* on its other. But there is more, for to stop there would again be to settle for eclecticism. And so, to prevent any final split, to continue to honor the elusive whole, reflection must strive to think the two together—with a "weighted focus" upon the former. Thus one appropriate representation of his thought is in terms of two overlapping circles, partially merged, with a certain emphasis upon one of the two: the figure of an ellipse.[9]

With these reflections as background, we may consider Ricoeur's early philosophy with a particular eye to the thematics of "the human" and "the whole." In so doing, we will want to have three books in view. *Freedom and Nature: The Voluntary and the Involuntary*, Ricoeur's initial venture in constructive philosophy, appeared in French in 1950. When *Fallible Man* followed ten years later, it was accompanied by a companion volume, an extensive study of religious symbol and myth entitled *The Symbolism of Evil*.[10] Later we shall consider how these books interrelate; for the moment it is enough to have the sequence in mind.

Throughout his early work Ricoeur draws particularly upon three philosophical mentors. We have already mentioned Edmund Husserl and we have noted something of the influence of Marcel; to these may now be added a third who is no less significant for being historically more distant, Immanuel Kant. Let us look more closely at how Ricoeur has appropriated and interpreted each of these three figures. Of the three, Gabriel Marcel (1889–1973) was perhaps the most immediate influence; he was in fact Ricoeur's teacher and *Freedom and Nature* is dedicated to him. Marcel, who spoke of his philosophy as a Christian existentialism, made classic a distinction between "problem" and "mystery." A problem is a question that can be resolved, generally by obtaining certain information. If the required data are not directly accessible, that does nothing to affect the nature of the question: it is still a technical puzzle to be settled on some future occasion. Observers often suppose that the role of philosophy is to serve as a kind of conceptual stopgap, speculating on such temporarily unresolved problems; and so they quite naturally conclude that philosophy is destined to be displaced by science. Against such notions, Marcel contended that the proper concern of philosophy was with certain intractable "mysteries" which are not subject to present or future resolution. A case in point is the inherently elusive relationship between the "lived body"—i.e., my body as my own, as the living center of my experience—and the same body regarded as a neutral object which might be objectively analyzed. Other examples are the irrational reality of evil, and, a theme underlying all the others, "the mystery of being." One needs no more than the titles of Ricoeur's early works in order to anticipate that *Freedom and Nature: The Voluntary and the Involuntary* was an exploration of the first of these mysteries, and *The Symbolism of Evil* was an exploration of the second. *Fallible Man* stands as the pivot between the two; and it is perhaps, of the three books, the readiest point of access to the question that underlies the others, the "mystery of being."

One must be wary of supposing, in this regard, that the concept of mystery is interchangeable with a particular experience—e.g., the experience of "the lived body." So directed, philosophies of a romanticist cast have set off in pursuit of an ever-receding point of inwardness—thereby losing sight of the very question Marcel had in mind, namely, *the relationship between* the lived body and the body-object. This is an instance of what Marcel describes, in another context, as something "which transcends any relationship properly so called, a *super-relationship* which it is not in my power to transform into a sort of ideal object, which I might mentally manipulate as one manipulates a formula."[11] As the awkward term "super-relationship" suggests, the reason this sense of inextricable relatedness is so important to Marcel is precisely because it offers our best clue to the underlying mystery, the nature of the whole. But it is a very peculiar sort of clue, whose implications are chastening; for if the mystery of my own incarnation is something that constantly eludes my grasp, surely the same must be true *a fortiori* for the mystery of being. And yet, on reflection, that is as it should be. For the whole, after all, is not an object which we can hold at arm's length to scrutinize and dissect. It is the reality *within which* we are constantly included, with which we are constantly involved. We are all prone to a sort of sluggishness of thought which would unreflectively assume that reality at large is "nothing more" than the sum of its analyzable parts. But if Marcel is correct, that is not true even of our own reality as incarnate beings, and so it is certainly not adequate as a way of addressing the mystery of being. "I cannot postulate an absolute totality, a complete and final whole, without putting myself, to some extent surreptitiously, that is, in a disguised fashion, in the place of the whole. . . ."[12] Similarly, we tend to think that the ambiguities of experience need to be ironed out before we can see things as they really are; but Marcel suggests that those ambiguities which arise from our own involvement are to be taken, *in their very opacity*, as the surest guides to the real.

Ricoeur, who follows Marcel in linking the notion of mystery to the question of the whole, derives thereby an important lesson for the encounter with reductionism. In briefest terms, it is the recognition that, truly to overcome reductionism, one cannot content oneself with simply opposing it. That is to say, it is not enough to assert, contra the reductionist, the element or aspect which the reductionist has neglected. For in advocating the part that has been neglected, we are still advocating a *part*, and thus we ourselves are well on the way toward fostering a reductionism of another sort. Simply to hold out for "freedom," for example, without making the effort to set forth an integrated viewpoint within which freedom may find its legitimate—and limited—place, is to substitute one abstraction for another. However laudable the intent, such one-sided fervor ends up by draining away the meaning of the very notion it wishes to uphold.

Accordingly we find in Ricoeur's first work, *Freedom and Nature*, not an assertion of freedom over against nature, in the manner of Sartre's philosophy, but rather a series of patient, concrete descriptions of the manifold ways in which the two aspects of experience interpenetrate and interact. Decision gives direction to the body; the body gives to decision a grip on reality and a source of affective motivation. There is a positive reciprocity; each realizes itself through the other. Similarly, *Fallible Man* begins with the crucial methodological affirmation that "the development of thought in a philosophical anthropology never consists in going from the simple to the complex, but always moves within the totality itself . . ." (4).[13] The point is crucial indeed: for once the final coherence of human experience has been surrendered, all the king's horses and all the king's philosophers will not put it together again. The sole remedy is *to begin from within* the fullness of experience, and to allow the various dimensions to unfold as aspects of that single fullness—ever aware that, because of its very fullness, it is a reality which constantly transcends us. This is undoubtedly the cardinal methodological lesson that Ricoeur drew from Marcel; its enduring character is apparent when Ricoeur concludes a recent discussion of his own philosophy with "the modest and uncertain formula that I borrow from Gabriel Marcel: 'I *hope* to be *in* the truth.' "[14]

Ricoeur's second mentor, Edmund Husserl (1859–1938), presents on first impression a marked contrast to Marcel. Whereas Marcel couched his insights in loosely textured, quasi-literary essays, Husserl's work is analytic and highly technical. Whereas Marcel warned against construing philosophy as a series of problems, Husserl wished to make of philosophy "a rigorous science." Yet Ricoeur is explicit that *Freedom and Nature* is to be located "at the meeting point of two demands: those of thought nourished by the mystery of *my* body, and those of thought concerned with the distinctions inherited from Husserlian descriptive method."[15] If Ricoeur has had any success in bridging the often unreconciled worlds of continental and Anglo-American philosophy, the reason may already be suggested in this early, twofold commitment to existential question and rigorous method. Ricoeur thus wishes to accomplish more thoroughly

than did Marcel himself the Marcellian project of "a second reflection": i.e., in Ricoeur's words, "the recovery of mystery in clear
thought, in a rigorous consciousness—in brief, in discourse."[16]

How, then, does Ricoeur propose to bring Husserl and Marcel together? We may anticipate that here too mediation cannot proceed
without some sense of an underlying affinity; and indeed one soon
discovers that the two do share, beneath the immediate contrast, a
common purpose. For Husserl sought in his own fashion to lead
philosophy out of the wasteland of one-dimensional thought. His determination to philosophize with greater rigor did not stem from a
placid belief that experience could be readily labeled and pigeon-
holed. Quite the contrary, the Husserlian method testifies to an
earnest conviction that a strict discipline of thought, an almost ascetic
self-criticism, is required in order to *prevent* us from slipping into
conventional, reductive modes of thought. The real threat is our own
complacent "natural attitude," which tends to coast along on custom
and cliché. Authentic experience, on Husserl's account, is not something that we simply "have" in pure, undistorted form; rather, we
find ourselves alienated from our own experience by a mass of assumptions about what is important, what is real. Our very sense of
the world is governed by unexamined assumptions, compulsive tendencies to pigeonhole, of which we are often unaware. The role of
philosophical rigor, then, is to lead us beyond these facile assumptions—not away from, but *toward* the spontaneity of actual experience. As Ricoeur says in another context, "consciousness is not a
given but a *task*."[17]

The meshing of Marcel and Husserl is legitimate, then. But more
importantly there is a sense in which it is quite essential, required by
Marcel's own concerns. We noted a moment ago how readily thought
slips away from the paradoxical coexistence of lived body and body-
object toward the celebration of the isolated experience of the lived
body as such. This tendency to rest content with an isolated concept
or an isolated experience, and thus shun the difficult path of "second
reflection," is not restricted to any particular movement; it testifies
to a common entropy of mind, and a common rigidity of character.
Thus far in our discussion we have focused upon the critique of
scientific positivism. But we have also seen that the mirror image of
positivism is a form of philosophical romanticism of which the
existentialists have not always been innocent. Ricoeur, for his part,

is emphatic that the problem extends well beyond any particular school of thought. It is the tendency, endemic to all of human thought, to avoid the risk of openness and otherness by seeking refuge "within the circle which I form with myself."[18] The image recalls the Lutheran definition of sin as the heart turning in upon itself, and the association is not inappropriate. For one cannot overstress the importance, for the development of Ricoeur's thought, of the struggle against philosophical solipsism in all its manifold forms.

Indeed, just to touch upon three dimensions of this struggle is to give a virtual summary of Ricoeur's methodology. First, Husserlian phenomenology prevents existentialism, Marcellian or otherwise, from becoming self-enclosed; for it requires a careful description that proceeds by way of the object. As Ricoeur cautions in the opening pages of *Fallible Man*, "reflection is not introspection; for reflection takes the roundabout way via the object; it is reflection *upon* the object" (18). The circle is opened, a second center is posited, thought moves through a larger arc—this is the procedure which Ricoeur sometimes calls "distanciation." While the introduction of Husserl's rigorous method provides an instance, distanciation itself is less a strict method than a characteristic turn of thought that reappears in various forms throughout Ricoeur's career. The practice may explain why Ricoeur often expresses himself in essayistic fashion, and why his thought is always so exploratory, so distinctly "on the way."

An instance of the more general use of distanciation, and a second aspect of Ricoeur's early method, is the application of this procedure to phenomenology itself. For Husserl's phenomenology risks a solipsism of its own, that of the "transcendental ego." Accordingly, in *Freedom and Nature* Ricoeur juxtaposes the results of phenomenology with those of the empirical sciences. The result is an illustration of the conceptual "ellipse" sketched earlier: the testimony of the empirical sciences must be at least partially incorporated into phenomenology—once again there is to be no facile eclecticism—but the result is a phenomenology that has been extended beyond its usual bounds. And here too one finds a larger lesson which proves applicable throughout Ricoeur's work; for the use of the empirical sciences in *Freedom and Nature* illustrates the fact that perspectives which, taken in isolation, might tend toward the reductionistic may actually become vehicles for greater openness when incorporated within a more encompassing movement or "detour" of thought. Striking illustrations in Ricoeur's later work are the incorporation of the Freudian "archaeology" within a larger teleology, and the appropriation of structuralism into a more comprehensive understanding of the literary text. It is through such detours of thought that "consciousness nourishes itself by recentering itself around its Other: cosmos, bios, or psyche. It finds itself by losing itself."[19]

But finally, even when supplemented and offset in this fashion—and indeed perhaps even *because* it has been so extended—reflection will tend toward the pride of self-sufficiency. Thus a third dimension of Ricoeur's method: it proves necessary to confront reason with an object so dense and inexhaustible that we can never pretend to have fully appropriated it. This is the function performed variously in Ricoeur's philosophy by symbol, myth, metaphor, and narrative: because they speak in a voice other than that of conceptual reflection, such texts may serve as both source and limit.

> "Symbol gives rise to thought." This maxim that I find so appealing says two things. The symbol gives: I do not posit the meaning, the symbol gives it; but what it gives is something for thought, something to think about. First the giving, then the positing; the phrase suggests, therefore, both that everything has already been said in enigma and yet that it is necessary ever to begin again and rebegin everything in the dimension of thought.[20]

Little imagination is required to link symbol, so understood, to the Marcellian concept of mystery. Of both it may be said that their opaqueness is their "very profundity, an inexhaustible depth." Each asks to be approached with a sort of respectful rigor by which the inexhaustibility will be, not reduced, but unfolded and affirmed. All of the Ricoeurian ventures in distanciation are occasioned by the self's tendency to close upon itself, which is simultaneously the tendency to reduce the other to an object that one can effectively grasp. But the whole that is testified in the various instances of symbol and mystery can never become object—it is rather the "*horizon*" within which we live, move, and have our being. To honor this horizon, a second reflection strives constantly to break open premature, objectivized notions of the whole; and it is in this effort that one encounters, most fundamentally, the coalescence of the two aspects of Ricoeur's thought that are represented by Husserl and Marcel. Once again what Ricoeur says of the symbol could be said of mystery as well: "the idols must die—so that symbols may live."[21]

II

With the notion of the whole as horizon, we touch upon the thought of the third of Ricoeur's mentors, the pivotal figure in modern philosophy, Immanuel Kant. But discussion of Ricoeur's appropriation of Kant is inseparable from the consideration of *Fallible Man*, and so it is to an introductory survey of the present book that we now turn.

In an early passage already familiar to us for its insistence that thought must not proceed "from the simple to the complex," Ricoeur sets forth his method for *Fallible Man*. Having affirmed that a philosophical anthropology "always moves within the totality itself," as an "elucidation of the global view," he proceeds to draw a conclusion very like that which we have noted in his discussion of the symbol:

> This totality, therefore, must first be given in some way prior to philosophy, in a precomprehension that lends itself to reflection. Consequently, philosophy has to proceed as a second-order elucidation of a nebula of meaning that at first has a prephilosophical character [4].

In *Fallible Man* the "nebula of meaning" is generated by "the *Pathétique* of 'Misery,' " an early section of the book that portrays human experience in terms of a certain chronic disproportion, a restless internal dissonance by virtue of which one never succeeds in coinciding with oneself. Thus through the imagery of disproportion the *pathétique* conveys something of the human totality—as paradox. The conceptual tension created by this synoptic depiction pervades the entirety of *Fallible Man*, mounting in intensity with each successive chapter. But within the pages of *Fallible Man* the tension never results in fracture; it continues to represent, in its fashion, a whole. So it is that the depiction of the *pathétique* set at the beginning of the book may succeed, in and through its very tensions, in providing a point of reference and a preconceptual corrective for all the necessarily analytic reflection that follows after.

Ricoeur's first step must therefore be to fashion a language with which to interpret the texts of the *pathétique*, and through which to draw from the text a sense of argumentative direction. The task is rather like that of the literary critic who develops a terminology with which to speak of the themes and continuities within a given text. This, then, is the role of Ricoeur's most obvious borrowing from Kant, the threefold structure of "finite," "infinite," and the mediation of the two.[22] The Kantian triad serves as a conceptual bridge across which the prereflective intuitions of the *pathétique* are able to inform the detailed, reflective discussions that make up the body of the book. By the same token, we must bear in mind that the language of finite and infinite is justified only insofar as it does succeed in serving as this conceptual bridge. The abstractions of "finite" and "infinite" are to be accepted neither on *a priori* grounds nor on the authority of Kant, but only insofar as they may be validated by the touchstone of the *pathétique*.

Once the framework of finite, infinite, and mediation is in place, Ricoeur is nothing if not consistent in implementing it. Indeed readers of a systematic bent may be inclined to schematize the entire book in terms of a simple conceptual grid. Moving laterally, one might project three columns representing a finite aspect, then a complementary infinite, and finally the mediation of the two. Then, proceeding vertically, three lines or levels corresponding to the three central chapters: "the transcendental synthesis" (sensibility–understanding), "the practical synthesis" (the will), and "affective fragility" (the emotions). Now, any schematic rendering of a complex work of philosophy can hope for no more than to find its place somewhere between the preliminary and the superficial. Yet it may be acknowledged that while Ricoeur is far from being a builder of systems, his thought does have a certain "systemic" character, so that a modest schema may be not inappropriate. Consulting the Contents, we find that the subsections of Chapters 2 and 3 arrange themselves neatly enough under the anticipated headings; and even within the more complex Chapter 4 we may discover that pleasure represents a finite aspect, happiness an infinite aspiration, and that there is posited a certain fragile mediation of the two. Judiciously employed, the schema will have its uses in helping us to keep bearings in the thickets of *Fallible Man*.

The crucial proviso is that we not use the schema in such a way as to construe *Fallible Man* itself as constructed out of so many conceptual building blocks—"from the simple to the complex." This misinterpretation is particularly tempting with regard to the successive chapters, which one might readily regard as treating various "faculties," understood as distinct compartments of the self. From that notion it is a short step to arranging the supposed faculties hierarchically, implicitly ascribing certain transcendent capabilities to the higher while subtly disdaining the lower as "merely finite." This is in effect what happens when the positivist places unquestioning confidence in the intellect, while dismissing the emotions as the breeding ground of bias and confusion; and when the romanticist retaliates by a simple reversal, disparaging the abstractions of reason in the name of the wisdom of the heart. In the face of this stale debate, the *pathétique* proves especially instructive; for it suggests that if the tension of finite and infinite is indeed fundamental, it is fundamental precisely because it does *not* correspond to the other, familiar distinctions and relationships within the self—but cuts across them all.

How, then, does Ricoeur proceed in his quest for an anthropology that will recognize the conflictual character of finite and infinite without giving way to the threatened fragmentation of the self? We shall content ourselves with five observations. First, *Fallible Man* understands itself as an exercise in "phenomenology": that is, the work tries simply to *describe* experience, without forcing the description to conform to extraneous suppositions about which of the various phenomena one encounters represent "the really real" and which do not. We commonly assume, for example, that in our experience of an object, the true or the objective is represented by the so-called "primary qualities" such as size and weight, features that can be strictly quantified. Impressions of color and lighting are deemed less important, and the object's emotional resonances may be disregarded altogether as being hopelessly subjective. Yet all of these are in fact aspects of the actual experience; and the moment we disregard dimensions of experience, we correspondingly diminish certain aspects of ourselves. "In this regard, phenomenology represents a return to naïveté. It liberates sight and renders it attentive to all the richness of the real."[23]

Still, distinctions do have to be made. Description cannot begin by saying everything at once. Thus a second point: within the whole, Ricoeur begins by "bracketing" certain aspects in order to concentrate on others. This act of bracketing is quite consciously a process of *abstraction*, not division: it gives us provisional *aspects*, not ele-

mentary parts. In this respect it is crucially different from the positivist procedure of going "from the simple to the complex." Knowing
that we are dealing with an aspect, we are reminded that we always
already function *within* an interrelated whole. Thus, for example,
perceiving and willing will be conceived as acts of the whole person,
not as isolated departments within the self. It does happen, however,
that certain aspects can be abstracted more readily than others; the
emotions, in particular, seem to be closely enmeshed in the concrete
totality of experience and the self. Accordingly Ricoeur makes a
tactical decision to begin the aspect that can most readily be abstracted and thus described: the "transcendental synthesis." This is
in keeping with his general philosophical proclivity for beginning
with the structural (cf. "eidetics") and proceeding to the more concrete (cf. "empirics"). The procedure is well justified as a way of
achieving an initial clarity—provided that we do not drift into thinking that, because it stands at the beginning and because it provides a
sort of paradigm for what comes after, the transcendental synthesis
is somehow the most real or the most basic of the several aspects of
the self.

Thirdly, when we follow Ricoeur's lead in beginning with the
transcendental synthesis, we quickly come upon his appropriation
of the Husserlian concepts of "noesis" and "noema."[24] Like so much
of Husserl's thought, these notions spring from the phenomenologist's
determination to find a way beyond the deadlocked disputes of metaphysics, or, more exactly, from his determination to undercut the
disputes by stepping *back* into what is nearest to us, the relative immediacy of experience. Traditionally, philosophical materialists have
contended that physical matter is the truly real, while idealists have
championed the primacy of mind. Husserl's strategy was to table or
set aside, at least temporarily, all such questions of what is ultimately
real, and simply to observe that in every experience there is in fact a
"noetic" and a "noematic"—roughly, a subjective and an objective—
pole. Further, Husserl observed that the two poles always appear in
correlation: no noesis without noema, no noema without noesis.
That is to say, there is no phenomenal object that is not an object
seen from a particular point of view, in a particular manner; and
equally there is no subjective experience that is not the experience of
some sort of object, whether it be deemed "real," "imaginary," or
whatever. Thus Husserl concluded that if one judges the traditional

philosophical disputes before the bar of experience, one finds no warrant for considering either pole more fundamental. Philosophy, he decided, would do better to get on with the task of carefully delineating the manifold ways in which, in practice, noesis and noema actually interrelate.

Ricoeur's debt to Husserl is nowhere more apparent than in the consistency with which his anthropology draws upon this noetic–noematic structure. Husserl's directive enables Ricoeur to show for example that the emotions, so far from being sheer confusion, actually exhibit a certain structure, and that this structure reflects the fact that a particular emotion always appears with reference to a particular object or noema. Conversely, the same procedure also enables Ricoeur to demonstrate his humanistic thesis that every object, even the most alien, always presents itself in relation to some particular noetic act. Yet for all this indebtedness to Husserl, Ricoeur effects a distinctive turn on the Husserlian method. For Ricoeur, as we have already noted, is sensitive to the fact that phenomenology is not exempt from the tendency of the self to form a circle closed in upon itself. For this reason, Ricoeur stipulates that, within the noetic–noematic structure, description must begin with the noema; only in a second, derivative moment is it then to reflect back upon the correlative noesis. Thus, for example, I do not know my finitude by a simple act of introspection, looking within myself. Rather I begin by noting that a given object presents only one side of itself: it is on this basis that I realize that I see things from a specific, limited point of view and am, in this sense, finite.

Ricoeur's over-arching intention, as we noted earlier, is to show how the fundamental tension of finite and infinite does not simply echo the familiar distinctions, thereby reinforcing them, but rather cuts across them all and thereby relativizes them. If now, as a fourth point, we consider how Ricoeur uses the structure of noesis and noema to accomplish this intent, we may anticipate that here, too, finite and infinite will not simply correspond with the given structure. Thus, for example, Ricoeur will not yield to the romanticist tendency which would suggest that the noetic, quasi-subjective pole is closer to the infinite while the noematic is inherently limited. Rather, the structure provides a way of showing that *every* experience has a certain limited, perspectival character, which presents itself *both* noetically *and* noematically. And similarly each experience has a certain infinite character, which Ricoeur locates initially in "the word"—i.e., in the fact that even as I see one side of an object, I understand it as, precisely, one side of a more encompassing object which I can in some fashion name. That name implicitly encompasses all the indefinitely numerous sides, aspects, and conditions of the object, actual or imaginable; and thus this remarkable capacity of language may be said to reflect the "infinite" character of our experience. To these reflections Ricoeur then adds a further proposal that anticipates his later writings on interpretation theory. He notes that the "infinite" character of language is not simply attributable to the subject who uses the language, affirming or not affirming what the language says. The "infinite" is to be found equally in "the objective moment of the *verb* that is significative by itself." Ricoeur enforces this point by positing a correlation of "assent" and "the verb," in which we find once again the familiar noetic–noematic structure. To give Ricoeur's passage in full: "if we link the subjective and volitional moment of affirmation to the objective moment of the *verb* that is significative by itself, there is no longer any distinction between two faculties or between an infinite will and a finite understanding" (36). This characteristic Ricoeurian point provides an occasion for noting that, while his use of the term "man" reflects a time less attuned to the need for inclusive language, the entire orientation of Ricoeur's philosophy—in its critique of hierarchy, in its defense of *praxis* and the affective life, and in its consistent advocacy of the wholeness of human experience—provides a significant resource for the rethinking of traditional patterns.[25]

Finally, we may recall that the real test of the Kantian notions of finite, infinite, and mediation is their efficacy in carrying forward into the body of *Fallible Man* the insights gained from the *pathétique*. Now, Kant's peculiar genius is to have fashioned "a philosophy of limits which is at the same time a practical demand for totalization."[26] And Ricoeur's own inspiration in *Fallible Man* is to wager that on both counts, as philosophy of limits and as practical demand for totalization, Kant's philosophy can provide the proper conceptual vehicle for the existential insights of the *pathétique*. To appreciate Ricoeur's thinking at this point we must note that, while the "limit" is often simply another term for the finite, there is also another level at which the concept of limit functions in *Fallible Man*. At this second level one may speak of limit—or "fallibility" or "fragility"—

with respect to *the relation between* the finite and the infinite, and more generally between the various aspects of the self. Thus, to quote Charles Kelbley, the translator of the present volume:

> The word "fault," at least in *Fallible Man*, should be taken in this sense as it is in the geological sense: a break, a rift, a tearing. Ricoeur frequently uses the words *faille* (break, breach, fault), which is akin to *faillibilité*, as well as *écart* (gap, di-gression), *fêlure* (rift), *déchirement* (a tearing, torn) to describe man's existential condition.[27]

Here the sense of limit becomes passionate—precisely because it is conjoined with a certain demand for totalization. In this regard we witness a progression that unfolds in the course of the work. The theme of non-coincidence first appears in quite moderate form within the transcendental synthesis, as an insuperable disparity between "intention" and "fulfillment."[28] It is exacerbated in the practical synthesis, and then is raised to an even higher pitch by the conflict between pleasure and happiness within the affective realm. But the most acute instance of fragility, perhaps, is to be found in a sort of existential trade-off that runs across Ricoeur's various chapters. For while the transcendental synthesis enjoys a certain stability, it lacks the gift of self-awareness; whereas the affective synthesis, which is endowed with a keen sense of self and of concreteness, must pay for the gift with an acute loss of stability. Nowhere does the self find an unambiguous response to its practical demand for totalization; everywhere it confronts the fact that, in Ricoeur's deceptively simple phrase, it is "only human."[29]

At the same time one finds in Ricoeur's very depiction of conflict a certain complementarity:

> For philosophical anthropology, knowledge and feeling (objectification and interiorization) are contemporary; they are born together and grow together. Man conquers the "depth" of feeling as the counterpart of the "rigor" of knowledge.[30]

The self thus displays a certain mobile-like complexity, its various aspects constantly in motion, constantly reflecting upon one another. Indeed it is hardly too much to say that the various aspects virtually "contain" one another: the transcendental synthesis represents the entire self—quite formally—and the affective synthesis embodies the whole—in a concrete and inchoate manner. From each of these shifting perspectives one glimpses the whole. And thus each perspective serves, in and through the details of its analysis, and in and through the tension or conflict it portrays, as a specific means of access to the abiding mystery.

III

As Ricoeur's own Preface to *Fallible Man* makes clear, the book was conceived as a contribution to a larger project begun in *Freedom and Nature* and continuing in *The Symbolism of Evil*. In the French, all three volumes were gathered under the comprehensive title *Philosophy of the Will*. At this time, Ricoeur's thinking was informed by debate with current forms of existentialism, particularly the writings of Jean-Paul Sartre. In the dualistic penchant of existentialism Ricoeur discerned a tendency so to elevate human transcendence that it became definitive of the genuinely human; and so to undervalue human finitude that it finally became fused with guilt. Remembering this period, Ricoeur subsequently reflected that:

> I had the impression, or even the conviction, that these two terms [viz., "finitude" and "guilt"] tended to be identified in classical existentialism at the cost of both experiences, guilt becoming a particular case of finitude and for that reason beyond cure and forgiveness, and finitude, on the other hand, being affected by a kind of diffused sense of sadness and despair through guilt.[31]

Thus there was what we may characterize as a "gnostic" drift in the thought of the period, which ran contrary to Ricoeur's own deepest inclinations as humanist and as holistic thinker. The multi-volume *Philosophy of the Will* may be regarded as Ricoeur's typically thoroughgoing response to these twin aspects of existentialism.

Freedom and Nature addresses particularly the first aspect, the over-valuation of human transcendence. We have already noted how this massive study traces, in case after case, the manner in which the voluntary and the involuntary are interlaced and interdependent. Across a spectrum of experience ranging from free decision to the "experienced necessity" of character, unconscious, and birth, Ricoeur argues that human transcendence, so far from being betrayed, is nourished and sustained by the involuntary or the finite.

To follow Sartrean existentialism in exalting transcendence at the expense of the finite is thus to pursue a will-o'-the-wisp. It is an instance of misplaced concreteness, or, worse perhaps, a case of misplaced humanity.

When *Fallible Man* and *The Symbolism of Evil* were published jointly in 1960, they shared a common title: *Finitude and Guilt*. One might say that whereas the "and" of *Freedom and Nature* had signaled a theme of interdependence, the integrity of freedom-and-nature, the "and" of *Finitude and Guilt* announced a programmatic contrast, as challenge to the second gnostic tendency, the conflation of finitude and guilt. Indeed the contrast was dramatized by the fact that the two parts of the single "volume" came separately bound, *Fallible Man* dealing particularly with finitude and *The Symbolism of Evil* dealing particularly with guilt. Yet even with this further development of Ricoeur's thought, the lessons of *Freedom and Nature* were not set aside. Here as elsewhere the suggestiveness of his philosophy arises from its being cumulative. Thus *Fallible Man* resumes, in a key more expressive of tragedy and conflict, the argument mounted in *Freedom and Nature*. It shows that even as viewed under the sign of the pathos depicted in the *pathétique*, and thus even as viewed in the terms most characteristic of existentialism, human experience continues to display the same recognizable interweaving of the finite and the transcendent, the finite and the "infinite." At the same time we also discover that even the extreme conditions of tragedy and conflict do not of themselves suffice to explain the actual occurrence of evil. Thus in *Fallible Man* the broadly phenomenological method initiated in *Freedom and Nature* arrives at its fullest realization—and a deliberate dead-end.

From this deliberate failure of method Ricoeur draws a substantive conclusion that secures his second line of argument against the gnostic despair. The limitations encountered by *Fallible Man* imply that by examining the structures of human existence one can delineate no more than certain *preconditions* for the occurrence of moral evil or sin. These preconditions are particularly apparent in the "fragility" or "frailty" which, as we have seen, are an important connotation of Ricoeur's "fallibility." But to be fragile is not yet to break: the impetus plunging us into moral evil is not generated by the structures of our humanity per se—and thus it cannot be blamed upon them. Finitude is not to be identified with guilt.

The positive lesson drawn from the incapacity of one method in *Fallible Man* is reinforced by the fact that when, in *The Symbolism of Evil*, Ricoeur does succeed in engaging the actuality of moral evil, it is by use of a different method that draws upon different sources. *The Symbolism of Evil* exchanges phenomenology for a hermeneutical method that looks to religious symbols, through which believers have confessed their complicity in evil. Ricoeur's study assumes at the outset the confession that is thus embodied in the symbols. The symbols function as a given, which cannot be explained adequately in rational terms, but which must be taken as a methodological starting point if reflection is to proceed at all. "By beginning with a symbolism already there we give ourselves something to think about; but at the same time we introduce a radical contingency into our discourse."[32] The result is indeed to create a hiatus between the two parts of *Finitude and Guilt*. For just as *Fallible Man* reaches "forward" only to the extent of delineating certain preconditions, still before the fact, so *The Symbolism of Evil* can probe "back" no further than the point represented by an irreducibly symbolic testimony, spoken after the damage has been done. The actual occurrence of moral evil falls "between" the volumes, as it were. In so doing it gives proof of its character as an instance of mystery, unmastered by the reflections of either.

In addition to the three works considered thus far, Ricoeur's Preface to *Fallible Man* anticipates a further, concluding study, a "poetics of the will." To date, that volume has yet to appear; in a sense one must reckon that it has been indefinitely postponed. The writings since *The Symbolism of Evil* have indeed amounted to a series of exercises in Ricoeurian distanciation, occasioned by the encounter with such "other" viewpoints as "the hermeneutics of suspicion," exemplified by Freudian psychoanalysis, and linguistic theory. But distanciation is always undertaken, as we have seen, in order to generate a larger, more encompassing perspective; and so it is possible to suggest that, in another sense, the series of seemingly disparate studies have not simply been a postponement, but have actually begun to constitute the anticipated "poetics of the will."

To see how this might be so, we need to pause for a moment of review, drawing particularly on Ricoeur's Preface to *Fallible Man*. We have touched repeatedly, in our discussion of Ricoeur, upon various thematics of the human and the whole. Within *Fallible Man* these thematics tended to focus less upon issues of ultimate wholeness than upon the wholeness of the human, the task of philosophical anthropology. But in the course of the effort to take account of the entirety of the human phenomenon, we were forced to recognize the extent to which the human is *not* whole, not finished and self-identical, but laced with tension and conflict. Thus there emerged in *Fallible Man*, and to a more acute degree in *The Symbolism of Evil*, the presentiment of "an obscure experience of non-being," which is the experience of evil. And in the very negativity of this experience, Ricoeur believes that it is possible to find, through "a kind of reverse participation," a mode of access to the mystery of the encompassing whole, the mystery of being. Following the French philosopher Jean Nabert, to whom *Fallible Man* is dedicated, Ricoeur urges that "it is this reverse participation that must be rediscovered, traversed, and surpassed by a reflection that would break through to what Nabert calls," in a phrase which we have seen to be quite fundamental to Ricoeur, "the 'primary affirmation' " (xlviii).[33]

Ricoeur clarifies the logic of this reflection when he speaks of "the grandeur and limitation of an ethical vision of the world," a phrase that, as he remarks, might have served as subtitle to *Fallible Man*. The ethical vision represents an effort to understand all of experience as related to, and in some sense deriving from, the reality of human activity. The grandeur of this vision is its readiness to shoulder responsibility for even those realities, such as certain instances of evil, which might seem most antithetical to it. Ricoeur might as readily have termed this the grandeur of the "humanist" vision. But in the very expansiveness of its effort, that brave vision is thrust up against its limits. Having affirmed that "evil comes into the world insofar as man *posits* it," the ethical vision is finally forced to acknowledge the other side of the reality of evil: that "man posits it only because he *yields* to the siege of the Adversary" (xlix).

It may come as a jolt to encounter this reference to "the siege of the Adversary," with its suggestion of a quasi-demonic power, in a work of philosophical reflection. We may remind ourselves, however, that this vision of humankind as "the victim of an Other" does not derive from such reflection per se, but comes from attending to the testimony of religious confession, in the manner of *The Symbolism of Evil*. Indeed the sense of conceptual incongruity and moral aversion that the notion occasions can be interpreted, on Ricoeur's terms, as a measure of the limits of the ethical vision. And yet there is within that vision, taken at its best, a profound recognition that anticipates the discoveries of *The Symbolism of Evil*. From the time of *Freedom and Nature* Ricoeur has insisted that every free activity is simultaneously an act of consent. Such consent is not to be confused with passivity; it is more nearly an *active receptivity*. Here we may have a clue to the "kind of reverse participation" that Ricoeur proposes to find in the most negative experience. Certainly the theme of an active receptivity proves to be a thread of continuity running from Nabert's "primary affirmation" through Ricoeur's early anthropology and on into his subsequent hermeneutical studies, with their quest for a "second naïveté."

The hermeneutical studies appear, in this light, as an extended detour by way of the object, where the object is understood as the manifold array of cultural representations—"the works, the deeds, the institutions, the monuments" and texts—in which human freedom has objectivized itself.[34] The detour is extended indeed, because these representations, as one soon discovers, give rise to a great variety of interpretations—the Marxist, the Freudian, etc. There quickly emerges a "conflict of interpretations" that is not unrelated to the conflicts already delineated in *Fallible Man*. Accordingly, the first task of hermeneutics is not to erect a grand theory of language, but to go about the more concrete, piecemeal task of mediating between colliding interpretations; and in the carrying out of this mediation, one continues to observe the characteristic Ricoeurian themes. As Don Ihde has remarked,

> In *Fallible Man* the third term is explicitly introduced as a limit idea. The dialectic of oppositions, limited in a third term, remains a hallmark of Ricoeur's method. *The third term, the struggle with a postponed synthesis, and the origin of the problem of hermeneutics are all one and the same problem.*[35]

With this remark we come upon what is perhaps one of the most stubborn issues in interpreting Ricoeur. Clearly the difficult mediation *between* conflicting interpretations is undertaken, not for its own sake, but in view of another, more fundamental mediation: that of a certain reality which can be known only *in and through* the oppositions. But what is the nature of that reality? On this cardinal question, Ricoeur's later philosophy would seem to point in two distinct, though related, directions. On the one hand, Ricoeur asserts emphatically that "reflection is the appropriation of our effort to exist and our desire to be, through the works which bear witness to that effort and desire."[36] Here hermeneutics is understood as being, finally, the mediation of self to self; "reflection is the effort to recapture the Ego of the Ego Cogito in the mirror of its objects, its works, its acts."[37] On the other hand, Ricoeur also holds it to be the task of hermeneutics to articulate "the world of the text," i.e., to find in the text a power beyond that of first-order reference, "another power of speaking *the world* . . . at another level of reality."[38]

It is not difficult to discern in this twofold account of hermeneutics the re-emergence, in another guise, of the humanist dilemma. It is a tenacious issue. If Ricoeur's work may be interpreted as a vigorous and many-sided meditation upon the implications of this dilemma, this can only be taken as evidence of the philosopher's determination to point beyond, to a vision of reconciliation. "By *Self*," he writes in a passage that is part report and part exhortation, "I mean a non-egoistic, non-narcissistic, non-imperialistic mode of subjectivity which responds and corresponds to the power of a work to display a *world*."[39]

For those who would enter into that compelling vision, there is no better place to begin than with the anthropology of *Fallible Man*—with its clear demand that introspective self-awareness must lose itself in order to find its self, and with its resolute delineation of "the grandeur and the limit" of the human.

NOTES

1. For further biographical details as well as an overview of Ricoeur's thought, see Mary Gerhart, "Paul Ricoeur" in *A Handbook of Christian Theologians*, edd. Martin E. Marty and Dean G. Peerman, 2nd ed. (Nashville: Abingdon, 1984), pp. 608–24.

2. Ricoeur, *Political and Social Essays*, edd. David Stewart and Joseph Bien (Athens: Ohio University Press, 1974), pp. 74–75. Cf. David Stewart, "Existential Humanism" in *Studies in the Philosophy of Paul Ricoeur*, ed. Charles E. Reagan (Athens: Ohio University Press, 1979), pp. 21–32. I am indebted to Stewart for noting the importance of Ricoeur's early essays. The volume of studies includes a useful bibliography.

3. Ricoeur, *History and Truth*, trans. Charles A. Kelbley (Evanston: Northwestern University Press, 1965), p. 328.

4. Gabriel Marcel, *Man against Mass Society*, trans. G. S. Fraser (Chicago: Regnery, 1952), p. 156. For Ricoeur's relationship with Marcel generally, see "Conversations between Paul Ricoeur and Gabriel Marcel" in Marcel, *Tragic Wisdom and Beyond*, trans. Stephen Jolin and Peter McCormick (Evanston: Northwestern University Press, 1973), pp. 215–56.

5. On behaviorism, see "A Critique of B. F. Skinner's 'Beyond Freedom and Dignity' " in Ricoeur, *Political and Social Essays*, pp. 46–67; on Freud, Marx, and Nietzsche, see "Religion, Atheism and Faith" in Ricoeur, *The Conflict of Interpretations: Essays in Hermeneutics*, ed. Don Ihde (Evanston: Northwestern University Press, 1974), pp. 440–67; and on structuralism, see particularly "Structure, Word, Event" in *Conflict of Interpretations*, pp. 79–96.

6. Mary Schaldenbrand, "Metaphoric Imagination: Kinship through Conflict" in Reagan, *Studies*, p. 79; the essay develops more fully a number of points that can be only touched upon in the present Introduction.

7. *Conflict of Interpretations*, p. 119.

8. Theodor Adorno, *Minima Moralia: Reflections from Damaged Life*, trans. E. F. N. Jephcott (London: New Left Books, 1974), p. 50.

9. Don Ihde, *Hermeneutic Phenomenology: The Philosophy of Paul Ricoeur* (Evanston: Northwestern University Press, 1971), p. 16.

10. Ricoeur, *Freedom and Nature: The Voluntary and Involuntary*, trans. Erazim V. Kohak (Evanston: Northwestern University Press, 1966); *Symbolism of Evil*, trans. Emerson Buchanan (New York: Harper & Row, 1967). Ricoeur's own précis of the three volumes of the "Philosophy of the Will" constitute Section I of *The Philosophy of Paul Ricoeur: An Anthology of His Work*, edd. Charles E. Reagan and David Stewart (Boston: Beacon, 1978). The second essay, "The Antinomy of Human Reality and the Problem of Philosophical Anthropology," is Ricoeur's distillation of *Fallible Man*.

11. Marcel, *Man against Mass Society*, pp. 124–25.

12. Ibid., p. 124.

13. References to *Fallible Man* will be given in parentheses in the text.

14. Preface to Reagan, *Studies*, final (unnumbered) page of Preface.

15. *Freedom and Nature*, p. 15.

16. Ricoeur, "L'homme et son mystère" in *Le mystère* (Paris: Horay, 1960), p. 120.

17. *Conflict of Interpretations*, p. 108.

18. *Freedom and Nature*, p. 14.

19. *Conflict of Interpretations*, p. 153.

20. Ibid., p. 288.

21. Ricoeur, *Freud and Philosophy: An Essay on Interpretation*, trans.

Denis Savage (New Haven: Yale University Press, 1970), p. 531; see also the helpful commentary of Patrick L. Bourgeois, *Extension of Ricoeur's Hermeneutic* (The Hague: Nijhoff, 1975), pp. 95–96.

22. Valuable insights into Ricoeur's appropriation of Kant may be gleaned from the latter half of his essay "Freedom in the Light of Hope" in *Conflict of Interpretations*, pp. 411–24; see also Schaldenbrand, "Metaphoric Imagination," pp. 60, 62, and passim.

23. Ricoeur, "Philosophy of Will and Action" in Reagan, *Philosophy of Paul Ricoeur*, p. 70.

24. For a basic orientation to these terms and to phenomenology generally, see Don Ihde, *Experimental Phenomenology: An Introduction* (New York: Putnam, 1977), and Richard M. Zaner, *The Way of Phenomenology: Criticism as a Philosophical Discipline* (New York: Pegasus, 1970).

25. Cf. "Fatherhood: From Phantasm to Symbol" in *Conflict of Interpretations*, pp. 468–97, and the section on having, power, and worth in Chapter 4 of *Fallible Man*.

26. *Conflict of Interpretations*, p. 413.

27. Charles A. Kelbley, "Translator's Introduction," below, p. xxxv.

28. Cf. the essay on "Kant and Husserl" in Ricoeur, *Husserl: An Analysis of His Phenomenology*, trans. Edward G. Ballard and Lester E. Embree (Evanston: Northwestern University Press, 1967), pp. 175–201; see also Ihde, *Hermeneutic Phenomenology*, pp. 60–61.

29. *Political and Social Essays*, p. 87.

30. "Antinomy of Human Reality," p. 32.

31. Ricoeur, "From Existentialism to the Philosophy of Language," *Philosophy Today*, 17.2–4 (Summer 1973), 89. The present discussion of *Philosophy of the Will* is adapted from Lowe, *Mystery & the Unconscious: A Study of the Thought of Paul Ricoeur* (Metuchen, N.J.: Scarecrow Press, 1977), pp. 11–13; the book contains a detailed examination of the conceptual structure of *Fallible Man*.

32. *Symbolism of Evil*, p. 19.

33. Cf. Ricoeur, "Nabert on Act and Sign" in *Conflict of Interpretations*, pp. 211–22.

34. *Freud and Philosophy*, p. 43. On the status to representation in the development of Ricoeur's thought, see Bourgeois, *Extension of Ricoeur's Hermeneutic*, pp. 99–105; also David Pellauer, "The Significance of the Text in Paul Ricoeur's Hermeneutical Theory" in Reagan, *Studies*, pp. 97–114.

35. Ihde, *Hermeneutic Phenomenology*, p. 16.

36. *Freud and Philosophy*, p. 46; italicized in the original.

37. *Freud and Philosophy*, p. 43.

38. Ricoeur, "Biblical Hermeneutics" in *Semeia* 4 (1975), 87; emphasis added.

39. Ricoeur, "Philosophical Hermeneutics and Theological Hermeneutics" in *Protocol of the Colloquy of the Center for Hermeneutical Studies in Hellenistic and Modern Culture*, ed. W. Wuellner (Berkeley: Center for Hermeneutical Studies, 1976), p. 17. For further critical discussion of issues of humanism and ontology in Ricoeur, see Lowe, "The Coherence of Paul Ricoeur," *Journal of Religion* 61.4 (October 1981), 384–402; the essay reappears with minor modifications in Lowe, *Evil and the Unconscious* (Chico, Calif.: Scholars Press, 1983), pp. 29–45.

TRANSLATOR'S INTRODUCTION

THIS ESSAY ON PHILOSOPHICAL ANTHROPOLOGY may, of course, be read apart from the author's other works. Yet the reader coming to Ricoeur for the first time will soon find that *Fallible Man* forms part of a vaster project which carries the over-all title of *Philosophy of the Will*. The project was initiated in 1950 with the publication of *The Voluntary and the Involuntary*,[1] followed in 1960 by *Finitude and Guilt*, of which two of the projected three parts have been published: *Fallible Man* and *The Symbolics of Evil*.[2] The purpose of this introduction is merely to situate the present work within the context of the general setting of the over-all project and to provide a brief sketch of its guiding intentions.

In his lengthy introduction to *The Voluntary and the Involuntary*, Ricoeur outlined the principal moments of his enterprise which we may characterize as diverse studies of, or approaches to, an understanding of the will and human existence. The first stage, *The Voluntary and the Involuntary*, is called an "Eidetics"[3] of the will, a method of "pure description" which abstracts from the factual in order to promote essence and meaning. One of the principal tasks of this first volume was to bring the descriptive method to bear on the reciprocity of the voluntary and involuntary aspects of man and to attempt to understand them. In abstracting from the symbolic, empirical, and poetic dimensions, Ricoeur hopes to reveal man's fundamental possibilities, the "eidetic" dimension. Yet the abstraction or "reduction" from these dimensions omitted two important factors from the descriptive analyses: "fault" and "transcendence." These two factors are treated, respectively, in *Finitude and Guilt* and in what had been projected as the third volume of *Philosophy of the Will*.

In *The Voluntary and the Involuntary*, we find that Ricoeur's problematic flows from somewhat diverging streams of thought: the phenomenology of Husserl and the existentialism of Marcel. While "meditation on the works of Gabriel Marcel is in fact at the root of the analyses of this book" (p. 18), it is complemented with the kind of distinctions coming from the Husserlian method of pure description. Thus we find a kind of interplay between Marcel's notion of the "Mystery" of the body as a subject and what Husserl called the "eidetic reduction." One could not, however, overplay Ricoeur's belief in the efficacy of "reduction," for, according to him, the understanding of the intentional structures of man's practical and affective life must have recourse to empirical and scientific data which serve as a "diagnostic" to these structures. Moreover, the basic relations of these structures reveal man's unity only by reference to the central "mystery" of incarnate existence. And so a true understanding of one's own body would seem to require active participation in our incarnation as "mystery." One must "pass from objectivity to existence."

Here, then, we find what might be called a mixture of "pure" and "impure" description, and what some may regard as the peculiar French modification of Husserl's phenomenology. Perhaps, however, the word "continuation" is the more appropriate. On the one hand, it was said in 1932 that Husserl's phenomenology is a philosophy of essences while Heidegger's is a philosophy of existence: "The philosopher's ego whence one starts in order to reach the meaning of being is the pure ego for Husserl; for Heidegger, it is the concrete human person. Perhaps the search for a philosophy of existence is precisely a reaction against Husserl's tendency to abstract from existence and everything concrete and personal."[4] Certainly French phenomenology, at least on the surface, would tend to corroborate this distinction. Yet in light of Husserl's "crisis period" it would seem that such a distinction is open to debate. Commenting upon the later Husserl, Ricoeur says: "In the works and unpublished papers of his last ten years, Husserl describes perception as the pre-existing soil and genetic origin of all the operations of consciousness. The consciousness which gives, sees, and brings about presences, bears and founds the consciousness which signifies, judges, and speaks. This change of accent marks the passage to existential phenomenology."[5] Needless to say, all of this enhances, as well as complicates, the ambitious attempts to answer the unrelenting question: "What is Phenomenology?" Suffice it to say that *The Voluntary and the In-*

voluntary has acquired a lasting place within the ranks of the phenomenological movement.

The publication of *Finitude and Guilt*, the second volume of *Philosophy of the Will*, marks the passage from the "Eidetics" to the "Empirics" of the will. In point of fact, the two parts of *Finitude and Guilt* constitute an introduction to and preparation for the empirical study which was to make up the projected third part. In this work, part of what was held in abstraction in *The Voluntary and the Involuntary* is introduced: the notion of fault. The first part, *Fallible Man*, is not concerned with the concrete manifestations of fault, whatever its form may be, but rather with that in man which permits fault to arise: fallibility. The word "fault," at least in *Fallible Man*, should be taken in this sense as it is in the geological sense: a break, a rift, a tearing. Ricoeur frequently uses the words *faille* (break, breach, fault), which is akin to *faillibilité*, as well as *écart* (gap, di-gression), *fêlure* (rift), *déchirement* (a tearing, torn) to describe man's existential condition. The same sense is provided by the verb "to err" (in the sense of wandering, going astray, deviating), which is retained in ab*err*ant and *err*or. This book, therefore, is concerned with that which allows for the possibility of a "rift" in man, what enables him to "err," become divided against himself and thereby to become the "flawed" creature.

The method used throughout the book is that of pure reflection, and while Ricoeur sometimes refers to this book as a "phenomenology of fallibility," it is undoubtedly more "constructed" than, for example, the phenomenology of Merleau-Ponty. In this sense there is an aspect of rationalism in Ricoeur's enterprise, a mode of thought which falls somewhere between Nabert's style of reflection and the phenomenological current of Husserl and Merleau-Ponty. Rationalism—if this is to say that the author seeks no radical point of departure—is involved in no frenetic search for the first truth. On the contrary, Ricoeur starts with the whole of man, the global dispositions of man's being that reveal his essential nature and the "disproportion" that leads to fallibility and the eternal schism in man.

This same point is perhaps best illustrated in *The Symbolics of Evil*, the second part of *Finitude and Guilt*, where the transition from fallibility to fault is effected. In *The Symbolics of Evil* Ricoeur starts out with the "fullness of language" and initiates a hermeneutics or exegesis of symbols and myths. The method is no longer that of pure reflection but is rather a confrontation with the fundamental symbols wherein man avows his *actual* fallen condition. Ricoeur, in making this recourse to symbols, believes that one is thereby enmeshed in the true immediacy of life. For beneath formal thought and speculation lies a more fundamental "language" whereby man first expresses himself: spontaneous ways of acting and thinking by which man understands himself in his world. We find, for example, that the experience of guilt, prior to a consciousness of evil, gives rise to a language, but one which is shot through with symbolism and, therefore, one which is in need of exegesis.

Neither the third part of *Finitude and Guilt* nor the third volume of *Philosophy of the Will* has been published, however, indicating a change in direction, or the manner of fulfilling, Ricoeur's itinerary. The question remains, where does philosophical thought go from there? As stated before, following these first two parts of *Finitude and Guilt* there was a projected third part, which was to formulate genuine philosophical anthropology, a truly empiric study of human volition, starting from the evocative power of the symbol. And according to the original, directive idea of *Philosophy of the Will*, the ultimate goal was to arrive at the "poetics" of the will, which would be developed in a third volume.

I want to thank the late Alden L. Fisher for reading through the entire manuscript and offering many suggestions and critical observations. Charles Courtney and Michael Kohn offered helpful comments on an early draft of the manuscript. I, of course, assume complete responsibility for any errors or inaccuracies.

CHARLES A. KELBLEY

NOTE TO THE REVISED EDITION

Apart from minor corrections and slight changes in language and style, this new edition remains substantially identical to the first.

CHARLES A. KELBLEY

Fordham University
June 1985

NOTES

1. *Philosophie de la volonté*: I *Le Volontaire et l'Involontaire* (Paris: Aubier, 1950).

2. *Philosophie de la volonté*: II *Finitude et culpabilité*: 1. *L'Homme faillible*, 2. *La Symbolique du mal* (Paris: Aubier, 1960).

3. The substantives *l'empirique, l'éidétique, la symbolique, la mythique,* and *la poétique* (empirics, eidetics, symbolics, mythics, poetics) are used in this Preface (with the exception of the last term), and elsewhere in the author's *Philosophie de la volonté*, to describe the various studies of or approaches to an understanding of the will and human evil. These terms are Germanisms and, excepting poetics and symbolics, as new to the English language as to the French. Since empiricism, symbolism, and mythology have other meanings and are associated with schools of thought, we have decided to follow the author's own terminology and use empirics, mythics, etc.

4. Edith Stein in *La Phénoménologie, journées d'études de la société thomiste*, September 12, 1932, p. 104.

5. "Phénoménologie existentielle," in *Encyclopédie française*, XIX (1957) no. 10, p. 9.

FALLIBLE
MAN

Preface

THIS BOOK IS A SEQUEL to *Le Volontaire et l'Involontaire,* which was published in 1950. The link between the present work and the preceding one, a phenomenological study of the project of voluntary motion and consent, has already been outlined in some detail in the introduction to the first volume (pp. 23–31). At that time I said that the present work would not be an empirical extension or a mere concrete application of the analyses that I then proposed under the heading of pure description. On the contrary, I said that I would here *remove the parentheses* in which it was necessary to put Fault and the whole experience of human evil so as to delimit the field of pure description. In thus bracketing the domain of fault, I sketched the neutral sphere of man's most fundamental possibilities, or, as it were, the undifferentiated keyboard upon which the guilty as well as the innocent man might play. Straightway that purely descriptive neutrality endowed all the analyses with a deliberately chosen, abstract turn. The present work intends to do away with this purely descriptive abstraction by reintroducing what was bracketed. Now, to take away the abstraction, or to remove the parentheses, is not to draw the consequences or apply the conclusions of pure description. It is to disclose a new thematic structure that calls for new working hypotheses and a new method of approach.

The nature of this new thematic structure and methodology was only briefly indicated in the introduction to the first volume. At that time we caught a glimpse of the connection between two guiding ideas. According to the first, the new description could be only an *empirics of the will*[1] that would proceed by means of a convergence of concrete representations; it could not proceed by means of an eidetics, which is an essential description, because of the opaque and

1. See Translator's Introduction n. 3 in regard to this term and others of like construction [Trans.].

absurd nature of fault. For fault, I said, is not a feature of fundamental ontology similar to other factors discovered by pure description, e.g., motives, powers, conditions, and limits. Fault remains a
foreign body in the eidetics of man. According to the second guiding idea, the passage from innocence to fault is not accessible to any
description, even an empirical one, but needs to pass through a *concrete mythics*. Thus the idea of approaching the empirics of the will
by means of a concrete mythics was already formed, but we did not
then realize the reasons for this detour. Indeed, why can the "passions," which affect the will, be spoken of only in the coded language
of a mythics? How are we to introduce this mythics into philosophic
reflection? How can philosophic discourse be resumed after having
been interrupted by myth? These are the methodological questions
that dominated the elaboration of that work.

This project of linking an empirics of the will to a mythics has
been specified and expanded in three directions.

First, it became evident that the *myths* of fall, chaos, exile, and
divine blinding, all of which are directly accessible to a comparative
history of religions, could not be inserted in their unrefined state into
philosophic discourse. First they had to be put back into their own
universe of discourse; for this reason I devoted several preparatory
studies to its reconstruction.[2] It then appeared that myths could be
understood only as secondary elaborations of a more fundamental
language that I call the language of avowal;[3] this language speaks of
fault and evil to the philosopher, and what is noteworthy in it is that
it is *symbolic* through and through. It does not speak of stain, sin, or
guilt in direct and proper terms, but in indirect and figurative terms.
To understand this language is to bring into play an exegesis of the
symbol, which calls for rules of deciphering: a hermeneutics. In this
way the initial idea of a *mythics* of bad will has been expanded to the
dimensions of a *symbolics of evil*. Now, in the center of this symbolics, the most speculative symbols, such as matter, body, and
original sin, refer to mythical symbols such as the battle between the
forces of order and the forces of chaos, the exile of the soul in a
foreign body, the blinding of man by a hostile divinity, Adam's fall,
and these refer to the primary symbols of stain, sin, and guilt.

2. One of them was published under the title "Culpabilité tragique et culpabilité biblique," in *Revue d'histoire et de philosophie religieuses*, 4 (1953).
3. *Le langage de l'aveu* [Trans.].

The exegesis of these symbols prepares the myths for *insertion* into man's knowledge of himself. In this way a symbolics of evil is an initial step toward bringing myths nearer to philosophic discourse. In the present work this symbolics of evil occupies the second of three projected books. Now, in this second part, linguistic problems hold an important place. Indeed, the specific feature of the language of avowal has appeared more and more as one of the most astonishing enigmas of self-consciousness—making it seem as though man reached his own depth only by way of the royal road of analogy, as though self-consciousness could be expressed only in riddles and would necessarily require a hermeneutics.

While the meditation on the mythics of bad will was unfolding into a *symbolics of evil*, reflection was pushing on in another direction: what is the human "locus" of evil, what is its point of insertion in human reality? In order to reply to that question I wrote the outline of philosophical anthropology placed at the beginning of this work. This study is centered on the theme of fallibility: the constitutional weakness that makes evil possible. By means of the concept of fallibility, philosophical anthropology comes, as it were, to the encounter of the symbolics of evil, just as the symbolics of evil brings myths closer to philosophic discourse. With the concept of fallibility, the doctrine of man approaches a threshold of intelligibility wherein it is understandable that evil could "come into the world" through man. Beyond this threshold begins the enigma of an upheaval in which discourse is only indirect and ciphered.

Just as the symbolics of evil represented an enlargement of the mythics proposed by *Le Volontaire et l'Involontaire*,[4] the theory of fallibility represents a broadening of the anthropological perspective of the first work, which was more closely centered on the structure of the will. The elaboration of the concept of fallibility has provided an opportunity for a much more extensive study of the structures of human reality. The duality of the voluntary and the involuntary[5] is

4. Two outlines of this philosophical anthropology have been published: "Négativité et affirmation originaire," in *Aspects de la dialectique* (Paris: Desclée De Brouwer, 1956), pp. 101–24; and "Le Sentiment," in *Edmund Husserl, Recueil commémoratif, Phaenomenologica* (The Hague: Nijhoff, 1959).

5. "L'Unité du volontaire et de l'involontaire comme idée-limite," in *Bulletin de la Société française de Philosophie*, January–March 1951; "Méthodes

brought back into a much vaster dialectic dominated by the ideas of man's disproportion, the polarity within him of the finite and the infinite, and his activity of intermediation or mediation. Man's specific weakness and his essential fallibility are ultimately sought within this structure of mediation between the pole of his finitude and the pole of his infinitude.

When beginning this work, by preceding the symbolics of evil with an elucidation of the concept of fallibility, I was confronted with the difficulty of incorporating the symbolics of evil into philosophic discourse. At the end of the first part, this philosophic discourse leads to the idea of the possibility of evil or fallibility, and it receives new life and considerable enrichment from the symbolics of evil. But this is achieved only at the price of a revolution in method, represented by the recourse to a hermeneutics, that is, to rules of deciphering applied to a world of symbols. Now, this hermeneutics is not of the same nature as the reflective thought that led to the concept of fallibility. The rules for transposing the symbolics of evil into a new type of philosophic discourse are outlined in the last chapter of the second part under the title "The symbol gives thought."[6] The text is the pivotal point of the whole work. It shows how we can both respect the specific nature of the symbolic world of expressions and think, not at all "behind" the symbol but "starting from" the symbol.[7]

The third part, which will be published in a subsequent volume, is devoted wholly to thought that starts from the symbol. It manifests itself in several domains, principally in the human sciences and in speculative thought. Today it is no longer possible to keep an empirics of the slave-will within the confines of a *Treatise on the Passions* in the Thomist, Cartesian, or Spinozist fashion. For a reflection on guilt, and one that is to do justice to symbolic modes of expression,

---

et tâches d'une phénoménologie de la volonté," in *Problèmes actuels de la phénoménologie* (Paris: Desclée De Brouwer, 1952), pp. 111–40.

6. "Le symbole donne à penser." In this section the author stressed the evocative power of the symbol, the "giving" or *donation* of the symbol: "The symbol gives; but what it gives is to be thought." See *La symbolique du mal*, pp. 323–32 [Trans.].

7. See "Le symbole donne à penser," *Esprit*, July–August 1959: "If we rule out finding a philosophy hidden beneath the symbol, disguised in the imaginative clothing of the myth, what is left is to philosophize starting from the symbol. The task of philosophy . . . is to promote and shape the meaning through a creative interpretation" [Trans.].

there is no by-passing the encounter with psychoanalysis, for such an encounter both is instructive and serves to define the peculiar intelligibility and the limits of the validity of this mode of reflection.[8] The evolution of criminology and conceptions of contemporary penal law can no longer remain irrelevant to our undertaking of extending the symbolics of evil into an empirics of the will. Likewise, we cannot afford to neglect political philosophy. When one has witnessed and taken part in the horrifying events that led to the hecatombs of concentration camps, to the terror of totalitarian regimes, and to nuclear peril, there can no longer be any doubt that the problem of evil is also intertwined with the problem of power.[9] Nor can there be any doubt that the theme of *alienation*, running from Rousseau through Hegel to Marx, has some connection with the accusation of the old prophets of Israel.

But if thought starting from symbols necessarily unfolds in the human sciences, psychoanalysis, criminology, and political science, it must also apply itself to the fundamental difficulty of finding a speculative equivalent for the mythical themes of fall, exile, chaos, and tragic blinding. This investigation cannot bypass a critique of the concepts of original sin, of the evilness of matter, and of nothingness. This investigation also leads to an elaboration of the speculative ciphers that can bring together, in the fundamental ontology of human reality, the description of evil as specific non-being, on the one hand, and, on the other, as a positive position. The riddle of the slave-will, that is, of a *free will that is bound and always finds itself already bound*, is the ultimate theme that the symbol gives to thought. Just how far such a speculative cipher of bad will is still capable of being *"thought"* is ultimately, from the methodological point of view, the most difficult question of this work.

The allusion to the theme of the slave-will gives us a glimpse of how much the foregoing problems of method are linked to problems of doctrine, to a working hypothesis, and to a philosophic stake. In

8. Reviewing Dr. Hesnard's books, *L'Univers morbide de la faute* and *Morale sans péché*, gave me the opportunity to outline this confrontation at a time when I did not foresee all the implications of the symbolics of evil. See " 'Morale sans péché' ou péché sans moralisme?" in *Esprit*, September 1954.

9. This theme is outlined in "Le paradoxe du pouvoir," in *Esprit*, May 1957.

order to designate this stake we could have chosen *Grandeur and Limitation of an Ethical Vision of the World* as a subtitle to this book. From one point of view this *recovery* of the symbolics of evil by philosophic reflection indeed tends toward an ethical vision of the world in the Hegelian sense of the term. But, on the other hand, the more clearly we perceive the requirements and implications of that ethical vision of the world, the more inescapable seems the impossibility of encompassing the whole problem of man and evil itself within an ethical vision of the world.

What do we mean here by an ethical vision of the world? If we take the problem of evil as the touchstone of the definition, we may understand by the ethical vision of the world our continual effort to understand freedom and evil by each other. The grandeur of the ethical vision of the world is to take us as far as possible in this direction.

To try to understand evil by freedom is a grave decision. It is the decision to enter into the problem of evil by the strait gate, holding evil from the outset for "human, all too human." Yet we must have a clear understanding of the meaning of this decision in order not to challenge its legitimacy prematurely. It is by no means a decision concerning the root origin of evil, but is merely the description of the place where evil appears and from where it can be seen. Indeed, it is quite possible that man is not the radical source of evil, that he is not the absolute evil-doer. But even if evil were coeval with the root origin of things, it would still be true that it is manifest only in the way it *affects* human existence. Thus, the decision to enter into the problem of evil by the strait gate of human reality only expresses the choice of a center of perspective: even if evil came to man from another source which contaminates him, this other source would still be accessible to us only through its relation to us, only through the state of temptation, aberration, or blindness whereby we would be *affected*. In all hypotheses, evil manifests itself in man's humanity.

It may be objected that the choice of this perspective is arbitrary, that it is, in the strong sense of the word, a prejudgment; such is not the case. The decision to approach evil through man and his freedom is not an arbitrary choice but suitable to the very nature of the problem. For in point of fact, evil's place of manifestation is apparent only if it is recognized, and it is recognized only if it is taken up by deliberate choice. The decision to understand evil by freedom is itself

an undertaking of freedom that takes evil upon itself. The choice
of the center of perspective is already the declaration of a freedom
that admits its responsibility, vows to look upon evil as evil committed, and avows its responsibility to see that it is not committed.
It is this *avowal* that links evil to man, not merely as its place of
manifestation, but as its author. This act of taking-upon-oneself
creates the problem; it is not a conclusion but a starting point. Even
if freedom should be the author of evil without being the root origin
of it, the avowal would place the problem of evil in the sphere of
freedom. For if man were responsible for evil only through abandon,
only through a kind of reverse participation[10] in a more radical source
of evil than his freedom, it would still be the avowal of his responsibility that would permit him to be in contact with that root origin.

This vision attained its first maturity with Kant's *Essay on Radical
Evil.* Moral formalism, in eliciting a single maxim of good will, also
brings out a single maxim of bad will. Through formalism, evil tends
to be reduced to a maxim of free will; it is the very essence of the
ethical vision of evil.

But the grandeur of this ethical vision is complete only when, in
return, we realize its benefit for the understanding of freedom itself.
Freedom that assumes the responsibility for evil is freedom that
comes to a self-understanding fraught with meaning. Before suggesting the richness of this meditation, correlative to the preceding one, I
wish to acknowledge my indebtedness to the work of Jean Nabert.
I found in his work the model of a reflection that is not content with
illuminating the problem of evil by means of the doctrine of freedom, but constantly enlarges and deepens the doctrine of freedom
under the sting of the evil it has incorporated within itself. In the
Eléments pour une éthique, reflection on fault was already combined
with a procedure oriented toward the apprehension of the "primary
affirmation" by which I am constituted as a self over and above all
my choices and individual acts. In this work, it became apparent that
the avowal of fault is, at the same time, the discovery of freedom.

The profound unity of the two temporal "ecstasies"[11] of the past

10. *Participation à rebours*—i.e., not a participating in *something*, or the
opposite of participation in the Platonic sense. See below on Nabert's concept
of fault [Trans.].

11. The French is *extases*. Cf. Heidegger's *Ekstasen* in *Sein und Zeit*, p.
329 [Trans.].

and the future appears primarily in the consciousness of fault. The forward *élan* of the project becomes overlaid with retrospection, while the distressed, remorseful contemplation of the past is combined with the certitude of possible regeneration; the project, enriched by memory, re-emerges as repentance. And so in the consciousness of fault, the future attempts to encompass the past, self-discovery shows itself as a recovery, and consciousness uncovers in itself a thickness or density which would not be recognized by a reflection attentive only to the forward *élan* of the project.

But in joining together the temporal "ecstasies" of the past and the future in the core of freedom, the conciousness of fault also manifests the total and undivided causality of the self over and above its individual acts. The consciousness of fault shows me my causality as contracted or bounded, so to speak, in an act that evinces my whole self. In return, the act that I did not want to commit bespeaks an evil causality behind all determined acts and without bounds. Where it is a question of a reflection attentive to projects alone, this causality divides itself in bits and fritters itself away in a disjunctive inventing of myself; but in penitent retrospection I root my acts in the undivided causality of the self. Certainly we have no access to this self outside of its specific acts, but the consciousness of fault makes manifest in them and beyond them the demand for wholeness that constitutes us. In this way, this consciousness is a recourse to the primordial self beyond its acts.

Lastly, the discovering through fault a discrepancy between the more profound demand for wholeness, on the one hand, and, on the other, duty and the acts that disappoint this demand, Nabert thereby detects in the consciousness of fault an obscure experience of non-being. He even goes so far as to make it a kind of reverse participation: any act whatsoever of the self, he says, "does not create by itself alone all the non-being that is in fault: it determines it and makes it its own. The non-being of fault communicates with an essential non-being that passes through the actions of the individual self without lessening the gravity of them for consciousness."[12] It is this reverse participation that must be rediscovered, traversed, and surpassed by a reflection that would break through to what Nabert calls the "primary affirmation."

---

12. Jean Nabert, *Eléments pour une éthique* (Paris: Aubier, 1943), p. 16.

Accordingly, in an ethical vision, not only is it true that freedom is the ground of evil, but the avowal of evil is also the condition of the consciousness of freedom. For in this avowal one can detect the delicate connection of the past and the future, of the self and its acts, of non-being and pure action in the very core of freedom. Such is the grandeur of an ethical vision of the world.

But can an ethical vision give an all-embracing explanation of evil? That is the constant underlying question in Nabert's last work, *Essai sur le mal*. If evil is the "unjustifiable," can it be wholly recaptured in freedom's avowal of it? I come to that difficulty in another way, in the *symbolics of evil*. The main enigma of this symbolics lies in the fact that the world of myths is already a broken world. The myth of the fall, which is the matrix of all subsequent speculations concerning the origin of evil in human freedom, is not the only myth. It does not encompass the rich mythics of chaos, of tragic blinding, or of the exiled soul. Even if the philosopher gambles on the superiority of the myth of the fall because of its affinity with the avowal that freedom makes of its responsibility, even if taking the myth of the fall as the central reference point allows us to regroup all other myths, the fact remains that the myth of the fall does not succeed in abolishing or reducing them. Moreover, the exegesis of the myth of the fall directly brings out a tension between two significations: evil comes into the world insofar as man *posits* it, but man posits it only because he *yields* to the siege of the Adversary. The limitation of an ethical vision of evil and of the world is already signified in the ambiguous structure of the myth of the fall: by positing evil, freedom is the victim of an Other. It will be the task of philosophic reflection to *recapture* the suggestions of that symbolics of evil, to extend them into all the domains of man's consciousness, from the human sciences to speculations on the slave-will. If "the symbol gives thought," what the symbolics of evil gives to thought concerns the grandeur and limitation of any ethical vision of the world. For man, as he is revealed by this symbolics, appears no less a victim than guilty.

1

The *Pathétique* of "Misery" and Pure Reflection

THE FIRST PART OF THIS WORK is devoted to the *concept of falli-bility*. In maintaining that fallibility is a concept, I am presupposing at the outset that pure reflection—that is, a way of understanding and being understood that does not come through image, symbol, or myth—can reach a certain threshold of intelligibility where the possibility of evil appears inscribed in the innermost structure of human reality. The idea that man is by nature fragile and liable to err is, according to my working hypothesis, an idea wholly accessible to pure reflection; it designates a characteristic of man's being. As Descartes says at the beginning of the fourth *Meditation*, man's being is such that "I find myself subject to an infinity of imperfections, so that I should not be surprised if I err." How man "finds himself subject" to err is what the concept of fallibility tries to make understood.

But how can this idea of man's fallibility be made clear? We shall have to be prepared to formulate a series of approaches that, although partial, will in each case grasp a global disposition of human reality (or the condition) in which this ontological characteristic is inscribed. My second working hypothesis, which now concerns the matter rather than just the rational style of the inquiry, is that this global disposition consists in a certain non-coincidence of man with himself: this "disproportion" of self to self would be the *ratio* of fallibility. "I should not be surprised" if evil has entered the world with man, for he is the only reality that presents this unstable ontological constitution of being greater and lesser than himself.

Let us go further with the elaboration of this working hypothesis. We are looking for fallibility in disproportion, but where do we look for disproportion? Here the Cartesian paradox of finite–infinite man recommends itself. Let us say at once that the connection that Descartes makes between this paradox and a faculty psychology is entirely misleading. Not only is it no longer possible to retain the distinction, at least in its Cartesian form, of a finite understanding and an infinite will, but we must also abandon the idea of linking the finite to one faculty or function and the infinite to another. For that matter, Descartes himself paves the way at the beginning of the fourth *Meditation* for a fuller and more radical grasp of the paradox of man when he surveys the dialectic of being and nothingness underlying the working of the faculties themselves:

> It is indeed true that when I think only of God, I am aware of nothing which can cause error or falsity. But on reverting to myself, experience at once shows that I am indeed subject to an infinity of errors, and on examining the cause of these more closely, I note that in addition to the real and positive idea of God, that is, of a Being of sovereign perfection, there is also present to me a certain negative idea so to speak, of nothing, i.e. of what is infinitely far removed from every kind of perfection, and that I am a something intermediate between God and nothingness, that is to say, placed between sovereign Being and not-being in such fashion that while there is in truth nothing in me, in so far as I have been created by sovereign Being, which can deceive me or lead me into error, yet nonetheless, insofar as I likewise participate in nothingness, i.e. in not-being, in other words, insofar as I am not myself the sovereign Being, I find myself subject to an infinity of imperfections, so that I should not be surprised if I err.[1]

We are certainly not in a position to deal directly with this ontological characteristic of man, for the idea of *intermediacy* that is implied in the idea of disproportion is also very misleading. For to say that man is situated *between* being and nothingness is already to treat human reality as a region, an ontological locality, or a place lodged *between* other places. Now, this schema of intercalation is extremely deceptive: it tempts us to treat man as an object whose place is fixed by its relation to other realities that are more or less

1. *Meditations*, IV, in *Descartes' Philosophical Writings*, trans. N. Kemp Smith (London: Macmillan, 1952), p. 233 (with minor changes in translation) [Trans.].

complex, intelligent, and independent than man. Man is not intermediate because he is between angel and animal; he is intermediate within himself, within his *selves*. He is intermediate because he is a mixture, and a mixture because he brings about mediations. His ontological characteristic of being-intermediate consists precisely in that his act of existing is the very act of bringing about mediations between all the modalities and all the levels of reality within him and outside him. That is why we shall not explain Descartes by Descartes, but by Kant, Hegel, and Husserl: the intermediacy of man can be discovered only via the detour of the transcendental synthesis of the imagination, or by the dialectic between certainty and truth, or the dialectic of intention and intuition, of significance and presence, of the Verb and the Look. In short, for man, being-intermediate is mediating.

Let us get our bearings before introducing any new elements into our working hypothesis: by allowing ourselves to begin with the Cartesian theme of finite–infinite man—even though we may have to reinterpret it completely—we dissociate ourselves to some extent from the contemporary tendency to make finitude the global characteristic of human reality. To be sure, none of the philosophers of finitude has a simple and non-dialectical concept of finitude; all of them speak in one sense or another of the transcendence of man. Conversely, Descartes, having announced an ontology of the finite–infinite, continues to call the created being of man finite with respect to the divine infinitude. Consequently it is unwarranted to exaggerate the difference between the philosophies of finitude and a philosophy that starts straightway with the paradox of finite–infinite man. But this difference is not trivial even when it is reduced to one of accent or tone. The question is whether man's transcendence is merely transcendence *of* finitude or whether the converse is not something of equal importance: as will be seen, man appears to be no less discourse than perspective, no less a demand for totality than a limited nature, no less love than desire. The interpretation of the paradox beginning with finitude does not seem to us to have any privilege over the opposed interpretation. According to the latter, man is infinitude, and finitude is a sign that points to the *restricted* nature of this infinitude; conversely, infinitude is a sign of the *transcending* of finitude. Man is no less destined to unlimited rationality, to totality, and beatitude than he is limited to a perspective, consigned to death, and riveted to desire. Our working hypothesis concerning the paradox of the finite–infinite implies that we must speak of infinitude as much as of human finitude. The full recognition of this polarity is essential to the elaboration of the concepts of intermediacy, disproportion, and fallibility, the interconnections of which we have indicated in moving from the last to the first of these concepts.

Our working hypothesis, however, is still not sufficiently formulated: it gives direction to the inquiry, but thus far no program of investigation. The question is how to begin. How can we determine the point of departure in a philosophical anthropology placed under the guiding idea of fallibility? We know only that we cannot start from a simple term, but must rather start from the composite itself, from the finite–infinite relation. Thus it is necessary to start from the whole of man, by which I mean from the global view of his non-coincidence with himself, his disproportion, and the mediation he brings about in existing. But is it not likely that this global view would exclude all progression and logical sequence? There remains the possibility that progress and order might develop in the course of a series of viewpoints or approaches that would in each case be a viewpoint on and approach to the totality.

Now, if the development of thought in a philosophical anthropology never consists in going from the simple to the complex, but always moves within the totality itself, this can only be a development in the philosophical elucidation of the global view. This totality, therefore, must first be given in some way prior to philosophy, in a precomprehension that lends itself to reflection. Consequently, philosophy has to proceed as a second-order elucidation of a nebula of meaning that at first has a prephilosophical character. This means that we must completely dissociate the idea of method in philosophy from the idea of a starting point. Philosophy does not start anything independently: supported by the non-philosophical, it derives its existence from the substance of what has already been understood prior to reflection. However, if philosophy is not a radical beginning with regard to its sources, it may be one with regard to its method. Thus, through this idea of a difference of potential between the non-philosophical precomprehension and the methodical beginning of elucidation, we are brought closer to a well-defined working hypothesis.

But where should we look for the precomprehension of fallible man? In the *pathétique of "misery."* This pathos is, as it were, the matrix of any philosophy that makes disproportion and intermediacy the ontic characteristic of man. Yet it is necessary to take this pathos at its highest point of perfection. Even though it is prephilosophical, this *pathétique* is precomprehension, and it is that insofar as it is perfect speech, perfect in its order and on its level. Accordingly, we shall look for some of those excellent expressions which tell of man's precomprehension of himself as "miserable."

Thereby the problem of a beginning takes on a new meaning: the beginning in philosophy, we were saying, can only be a beginning in elucidation whereby philosophy recommences rather than commences. In order to reach this methodical beginning, we will have to bring about a reduction of the *pathétique* at the beginning of the next chapter and initiate an anthropology that is genuinely philosophical. This will be done by means of a reflection of a "transcendental" style, i.e., a reflection that starts not with myself but with the object before me, and from there traces back to its conditions of possibility. I shall consider the characteristics of this "transcendental" style later on; let me say here only what I expect from this decision to look within the power of knowing for man's most radical disproportion. From it I seek a clue to the exploration of all the other modalities of man as intermediate: what was mélange and misery for the pathetic comprehension of man will be called "synthesis" in the object; the problem of the intermediate will become that of the "third term," which Kant called "transcendental imagination" and which is discovered reflectively *on* the object. Without this transcendental stage, philosophical anthropology would quit the *pathétique* only to fall into a fanciful ontology of being and nothingness.

With this twofold beginning, prephilosophical and philosophical, pathetic and transcendental, we are provided with the elements for going on. The transcendental stage furnishes only the first stage of a philosophical anthropology and does not take in everything of which the *pathétique* of misery is the precomprehension. All that follows in this philosophy of fallibility will consist in progressively filling in this gap between the *pathétique* and the transcendental, in recovering philosophically the whole rich substance that does not enter into transcendental reflection based on the object. This is why we shall try to fill the gap between *pure* reflection and *total* comprehension by means of a reflection on "action" and then on "feeling." Yet transcendental reflection on the subject can still serve as a guide in these two new ventures; for we can reflect on the new forms presented by man's non-coincidence with himself in the orders of action and feeling only in terms of the disproportion between Reason and Sensibility, or, as I shall presently and more accurately express it, between the Word and Perspective. Likewise, if we take the mediation of the transcendental imagination as a model, we can understand the new forms that the intermediary or mediating function acquires in the practical and affective orders.

Thus it appears reasonable to attempt a progressive recovery of the initial *pathétique* of "misery" by pure reflection. The whole movement of this book consists in an attempt to enlarge reflection step by step, beginning with an initial position of a transcendental style. At the extreme limit, pure reflection, by becoming total comprehension, would be equivalent to the *pathétique* of misery.

But this limit is never attained, because in man's precomprehension of himself there is a wealth of meaning that reflection is unable to equal. This residue of meaning will force us to attempt an entirely different approach in Book II: no longer by pure reflection but by an exegesis of the fundamental symbols in which man avows the servitude of his free will.

The first book will take the reflective style to its utmost point: from the disproportion of knowing to that of acting and from that of acting to that of feeling. At this point, where reflection can no longer expand, it will be possible to experience the real import of the concept of fallibility: indeed, fallibility constitutes the regulative idea of this movement of thought which attempts to make the rigor of reflection equal to the richness of the pathetic comprehension of misery.

THE PATHÉTIQUE OF "MISERY"

On two occasions, with Plato and Pascal, this meditation on pathos dawned on the margins of philosophy, and on the threshold, as it were, of a reflection that would invest it with rigor and truth. We can detect a certain progression in going from the Platonic myth representing the soul as a mélange to the beautiful Pascalian rhetoric of two Infinites toward Kierkegaard's *Concept of Dread*. This is at once a progression in the pathetic dimension as well as in the precomprehension of "misery." This progression, however, develops in the very interior of images, figures, and symbols, and it is through these that pathos reaches mythos, which is already discourse.

The whole precomprehension of "misery" is already to be found in the myths of the *Symposium*, the *Phaedrus*, and the *Republic*. The myth is the misery of philosophy; but philosophy, when it wishes to speak of man, and not of the Idea which is and which gives measure to all being, is the philosophy of "misery." Indeed, it is the very situation of the miserable soul. Inasmuch as the soul is the intermediate being *par excellence*, it is not Idea: at the very most it is "of the race of Ideas" and is what is "closest" to the Idea. But neither is it a perishable thing: its body is what "most resembles" the corruptible. The soul, however, is the very movement from the sensible toward the intelligible; it is *anabasis*, the rising toward being; its misery is shown in that it is at first perplexed and searches (ἀπορεῖν καὶ ζητεῖν).[2] This perplexity, this aporia, and this quest, which are reflected in the very incompletion of the aporetic dialogues, show that the soul is in development with respect to being. The soul holds opinions and makes mistakes; it is not vision, or at least not at first, but an aim. It is not contact and possession, not at the very first, but tendency and tension: "With time and effort and through a long and difficult process of schooling" says the *Theaetetus* (186a).

How are we to *tell of* the soul and its function of transition between that which passes away and that which abides? Unable to speak of it in the language of Science, i.e., in the immutable discourse on immutable Being, the philosopher expresses it in the language of allegory, and then in the language of myth.

Allegory, analogy will suffice to give a temporarily stable image of this strange becoming without philosophic status, ἄτοπος. Thus Book IV of the *Republic* gives a political symbol of the soul according to which the soul is composed of three parts, just as the City is made up of three orders: Rulers, Auxiliaries, and Craftsmen. This symbolism falls short of myth as long as this static image is not put back into motion in the perspective of the *élan* toward the Ideas and toward the Good and, consequently, as long as the *genesis* of this multiple unity is not evoked with regard to the *anabasis* that leads back to being and the Good. But the visualization of the "becoming"

2. *Republic* 523a–525a.

of the soul is watermarked, so to speak, within the immobilized image. At the very beginning of the comparison Plato says: "Suppose we imagine the forming of a state [γιγνομένην πόλιν]. Would we not also see justice *take form* [γιγνομένην] there as well as injustice?"[3] Justice is nothing else than this form of unity in the movement of the parts: it consists essentially in "becoming the unity of the many" (ἕνα γενόμενον ἐκ πολλῶν).[4]

But the fourth book proceeds straightway to the supposedly realized term of this synthesis: if the State is rightly constituted it is perfectly good; then it is wise, courageous, temperate, and just. This order, taken in its accomplished state, displays the tripartite structure, each of the virtues settling in one "part" of the City. Therefore, each of the parts of the soul is, like those of the City, the seat of a function. In turn, the balance of the three functions making up the soul's structure derives from the supposedly realized norm of justice: justice is "that which makes it possible for the three functions to come into being and so long as it remains present secures their continuance."[5]

But if we view the soul in its very movement toward unity and order instead of proceeding by imagination to the terminus of the movement by which the State is established, then the image comes to life. Instead of a well-balanced structure, it is a non-determined movement, a system of tensions that emerges. This shift is very perceptible in the continuation of Book IV when, abandoning the image of the well-established City, Plato considers the powers by which we "act," that is to say, by which we "learn," "feel anger," and "desire." Then the soul appears as a field of forces undergoing the double attraction of reason called "that which urges" (τὸ κελεῦον) and of desire which is characterized as "something that holds back" (τὸ κωλῦον: 439c). That is where the third term, the one Plato calls θυμός, becomes enigmatic. It is no longer a "part" in a stratified structure, but an ambiguous power which undergoes the double attraction of reason and desire. Sometimes it battles along with (ξύμμαχον) desire in the form of irritation and fury; sometimes it takes the side of reason in the form of indignation and endurance. "Anger" or "courage," the θυμός, the heart, is the unstable and fragile function

3. Ibid. 369a.
4. Ibid. 443a.
5. Ibid. 433b.

par excellence. This ambiguous situation of the θυμός evinces, in a "static" representation of the soul, all the myths of intermediacy. In a static representation the intermediate is a "mean," it is "between" two other functions or parts. In a dynamic representation it will be a "mélange." But allegory, which was still suitable for a static representation, points beyond itself to myth, which alone is able to tell of the genesis of the intermediate.

The image of mélange, applied to the soul, gives the dramatic form of a narrative to the more static theme of the tripartite composition. Accordingly, we need a myth to relate the genesis of the mélange. Occasionally this will be the myth of artifaction, of an alloying of materials, often the biological myth of an alliance, of a coupling between the sexed terms; γένεσις is then γέννησις, genesis is generation. This mélange, in the form of an alloying or coupling, is the event that took place at the origin of souls.

That which puts the myths of the *Symposium* and the *Phaedrus* at the head of the non-philosophical or prephilosophical representations of an anthropology of fallibility is not only their historical antecedence, but the *undifferentiated* character of the theme of "misery" that they convey. In them misery is indivisibly both primordial limitation and original evil. We may read these great myths successively as a myth of finitude on the one hand; of guilt, on the other. The myth is a nebula that reflection will have to break down. A more direct reflection on the myths of evil will later reveal to what mythical foundation this nebula of miserable existence and fallen freedom belongs. We shall also see that Plato, the philosopher, did not confuse evil with bodily existence, and that in Platonism there is an evil of injustice, an evil peculiar to the soul.

If we take the myth as it is told, that is, without the background that the history of religions can restore and without the exegesis that begins to break it down, it is a global myth of "misery." And we may say that every meditation comes back to the theme of misery when it restores this indivision of limitation and moral evil. "Misery" is that undivided disgrace which the myths of mélange tell of before ethical reflection comes along and reduces it to "body" and "injustice."

It is true that the inspired priestess does not speak of the soul, but of Eros, demi-god, demon. Eros, however, is himself a representation of the soul—or at least of the soul that is most soul, that of the philosopher who desires the good because he is not in himself the Good. Now, Eros carries in himself that original wound which is the emblem of his mother, Penia. And this is the principle of opacity. To account for the aspiration for being, we need a root of indigence, of ontic poverty. Eros, the philosophizing soul, is therefore the hybrid *par excellence*, the hybrid of Richness and Poverty.

Descartes and especially Kant say the same thing in their judicious treatises on the imagination: the understanding without intuition is empty, intuition without concepts is blind. The light of the imagination is their synthesis: the Platonic hybrid bespeaks the transcendental imagination; it foreshadows it in that it includes every generation by the body and the mind, what the *Philebus* calls, in a less "mythical" and more "dialectical" language, the "coming into existence," the γένεσις εἰς οὐσίαν, which is, moreover, a "generated essence."[6] All creation, all ποίησις, is an effect of Eros: "The idea of creation, as you know, can be taken in many ways. For the cause of anything whatever that emerges from non-being into being is always an act of creation."[7] In short, Eros is the law of every *work* that is richness of Meaning and poverty of brute Appearance. That is why the ascending dialectic, which marks out a love that is ever purer, traverses all the stages of the work, from beautiful bodies to beautiful souls, to beautiful actions and legislations. Every work is born of desire, and every desire is both rich and poor.

But there is more in myth than in reflection: myth has more in potential even if it is less determinate and less rigorous. This inexhaustible reserve of meanings is not only in Poros, which is quite obviously more and better than the Kantian conception of the understanding, but also in Penia.

Every indigence is Penia, and there are many ways of being poor. In fact, if we elucidate the myths of the *Symposium* and the *Phaedrus* one by the other, the indetermination or the over-determination of the first stands out clearly. Ontic indigence, represented by Penia in the *Symposium*, begins to divide into two mythical moments that correspond to two different phases of the narrative in the *Phaedrus*.

6. *Philebus* 26d–27b [Trans.: at this point in the *Philebus*, Plato is speaking of the two classes of the infinite and the finite, and their "offspring," the third class, which is a combination of the first two, or a generated essence or mixture (*essence devenue*)].

7. *Symposium* 205b–c.

In point of fact, the *Phaedrus* links a myth of fragility to a myth of downfall; the fragility that precedes every fall is that of those teams of winged horses in the celestial procession which represent human souls. Prior to any fall, those souls are already composed, and their composition conceals a point of discord in the team itself: "The charioteer of the human soul drives a team, and one of the horses is beautiful, good, and formed of such elements, whereas the make-up of the other one is quite the opposite" (ὁ δ'ἐξ ἐναντίων τε καὶ ἐναντίος).[8] Thus, before the fall into a terrestrial body, there is a primordial incarnation: in this sense the gods themselves have a body, but the body of the non-divine souls contains an inherent principle of heaviness and obstinacy. And the myth of fallibility, in the chiaroscuro and ambiguity, turns into a myth of fall. The teams mutually impede each other and founder in the eddies. The Wing which gave rise to the soaring climb crumples and falls. Then the soul is dimmed by its forgetfulness of Truth: from now on man will feed on opinion.

In this sliding from fragility to vertigo and from vertigo to the fall, the Platonic myth foreshadows the Kierkegaardian meditation which will also waver between two interpretations of the birth of evil in innocence, where evil is at one time interpreted as a continuity and at another as a discontinuity, but in the end turning toward the idea that evil is an upheaval, a leap, a positing. In this sense the Platonic myth of misery is a nebula of fragility and downfall which begins to split up, but which remains undivided and tentative. Plato calls this nebula "disgrace," "forgetfulness," and "perversion."[9]

Later on we shall show how Plato caught a glimpse of the passage from myth to dialectic and how the *mélange* becomes the *mixture*, then the *absolute mean*.[10] As we shall see, this takes place by means of a transposition of the Pythagorean opposition between the Limit and the Unlimited as well as with the aid of practical reason.

The Pascalian *pathétique* provides us with the second reflective beginning: the celebrated sections entitled "Two Infinites, the mean"

8. *Phaedrus* 246b.
9. Ibid. 248c.
10. The author is alluding to Plato's various representations of the soul: as a tripartite "composition" (*Republic, Phaedrus, Timaeus*), as a "mélange" of disparate elements (*Symposium, Gorgias*), as a harmonious "mixture" or blending of reason and desire (*Philebus*), and the "absolute mean" (*la juste mesure*) as exemplified in virtue and art (*Politicus*) [Trans.].

or "Man's Disproportion" (pen. 72 in Brunschvicg's edition) are of another order as much by their intention as by their tone. The tone is not that of myth but of rhetoric. On the Platonic scale of knowledge it would be an exhortation or an *apologia*, or, in other words, a straightforward opinion. The *Phaedo*, which also begins with an exhortation, even speaks in this sense of "persuasion [παραμυθία] and proof" (70b). Indeed, by using a kind of persuasion, Pascal invites us to forgo diversion and to pierce the veil of pretense by which we hide from our true situation. Brunschvicg understood very well that it was not necessary to separate this meditation on man as situated between two infinites from the "chapter on the deceptive powers" (pen. 83), imagination and habit, which leads straight to the critique of distraction. To reflect on the place of man as an intermediate being is to return to myself in order to "think about what it is to be a king and to be a man" (pen. 146).

This meditation remains an *apologia* or a *paramythia* because it starts from a purely spatial schema of man's place among things. This representation of the "place"[11] of man is wholly imaginative, and portrays him as being intermediate between the very great and the very small. It has, however, the advantage of affecting man because it awakens an immediate echo in the cosmological sensibility of a century engaged in discovering the vastness of the universe: "What is a man in the infinite?" This is the view, extended by the imagination, that nourishes the emotion of a man who "regards himself as lost in this remote corner of nature; . . . but if our view stops here, let the imagination pass on; it will exhaust its powers of thinking long before nature ceases to supply it with material for thought" (pen. 72). Astronomy, science, comes in "to inflate our conceptions," but what it proposes beyond the imaginable only serves to astonish the imagination until it "loses itself in that thought." Then the imagined infinite becomes an "abyss," and a double abyss. The very word infinite is more expressive than meaningful. It does not and could not denote a concept of reason, for it is rather indefinite as to greatness and smallness than a reference to infinity and nothingness. The words infinite and nothingness, fraught with dread, rather manifest the astonishment of the imagination which exhausts its powers of

11. The French *lieu*, which is found in the word *milieu*. The author refers to man's place (*lieu*) in nature as the "mean" (*milieu*), and to man as the being of the mean (*l'être du milieu*) or the intermediate being [Trans.].

thinking and stands in amazement before these marvels: "For after all, what is man in nature? A nothing in comparison with the infinite, an all in comparison with nothing, a mean between nothing and all."

The awakening power of the spatial symbolism of the two infinites consists in giving rise to its own transcendence toward a properly existential schema of disproportion: "Limited as we are in every way, this state which is between two extremes pervades all our functions" (pen. 72). Each of the extreme terms gradually becomes charged with meaning, as by a Platonic reminiscence on all the analogies between the sensible and the intelligible. The infinitely great, the infinite itself, becomes the "end of things," that toward which all things are "borne." The infinitely small, also called nothingness, becomes the "principle" hidden from man, and again, "the nothingness from which he came": "All things emerge from nothingness and are borne toward the infinite." Here, then, is man situated between the origin and the end, in a sense that is at once temporal, causal, and teleological. And his disproportion consists in that he does not at all have the "infinite capacity" to "understand" or to embrace the principle and the end.

As nature has "engraved her image and that of her Author on all things," this double infinity of things is repeated in the sciences themselves. The nothingness of origin is reflected in the problem of the point of departure in science. That the final purport of the sciences eludes us, we admit; but that the principles are a sort of infinity of smallness and even of nothingness is less common knowledge. This upsets our belief in a simple point of departure. There is no simple idea, simple being, a monad from which one can start. The principles are to the understanding what the infinitely small is to the conception of our imagination, a kind of nothingness: now "we need no less capacity to attain nothingness than to attain the all." The whole question of the sense of subtlety[12] and the principles sensitive to the heart has its point of insertion here.

Is this "misery," which is comparable to the wandering of mortals in Parmenides' *Poem* or to the unstable and changing opinion found in Plato, thus a primal wound in the human condition, or is it our fault? Is the nebula of limitation and evil, which the *Phaedrus* did not clearly separate, going to break up?

12. Pascal's *l'esprit de finesse* [Trans.].

Still not clearly. "Misery" still remains an undivided theme. In fact, it is noteworthy that man's very situation between the extremes is depicted as in itself dissimulating: "Then let us learn our range: we are something but we are not everything. Whatever existence we have hides from us the knowledge of the first principles that arise out of nothingness; and the smallness of our being hides from us the sight of the infinite. . . . This is our natural condition, and yet more contrary to our inclination" (pen. 72). Likewise: "But when, on a stricter examination, after finding the cause of all our ills, I tried to discover the reason behind it, I found that there is one very real reason: the natural poverty of our weak and mortal condition, so miserable that nothing can comfort us when we dwell on it" (pen. 139).

And yet diversion is our fault; if it is not, then why this exhortation: "Let us learn our range"? "Weak," "powerless," "inconstant," "ridiculous," man is not such that he does not have the responsibility of knowing himself: "It is certainly an evil to be full of faults; but it is a still greater evil to be full of them and to refuse to recognize them, since that is to add the further fault of voluntary illusion" (pen. 100). Accordingly, in order to give an explanation of diversion we must turn to a certain "aversion to truth" (pen. 100), which, although having "a natural root in his heart" (pen. 100), is nevertheless a very deliberate work, an illusory stratagem, a preventive maneuver with respect to this woe of woes which would be to find oneself miserable. This stratagem, which Pascal calls a "secret instinct," therefore involves a natural feeling of man's miserable condition, no sooner conceived than banished: "a sense of their constant misery," says Pascal (pen. 139). This "sense" supposes "another secret instinct, a remnant of the greatness of our primitive nature, which teaches them that happiness in reality consists only in rest and not in turmoil. And from these two contrary instincts they form within themselves a confused project, hidden from view in the depths of their soul, impelling them to pursue repose through excitement, and always to imagine that the satisfaction that they do not have will come to them if, by surmounting whatever difficulties confront them, they can open the door to rest" (pen. 139).

Thus the meditation of Pascal starts with a wholly external imagination of the spatial disproportion of man which reflects itself in a view of the disproportion of knowledge about things. In its turn, this disproportion becomes interiorized in the theme of the dissimulation that man's finite condition secretes and, as it were, exudes with regard to the question of origin and end. In short, this very dissimulation appears as the paradox and the vicious circle of bad faith. The human condition is naturally dissimulating in regard to its proper significance. But this dissimulation is—also and nevertheless—the work of the diversion that the rhetoric of the "two infinites" and the "mean" would render veracious.

The rhetoric of misery does not seem able to go beyond this paradox of a dissimulating–dissimulated condition. At the level of exhortation, of the Pascalian persuasion, its ambiguity remains. And this paradox must keep all the appearances of a vicious circle.

It is now the task of pure reflection to understand fallibility and, in understanding it, to break down the nebula of "misery" into distinct forms.

2

The Transcendental Synthesis

THE *pathétique* OF MISERY gives philosophy the substance of its meditation but not its point of departure. How can we pass from the myth of "mélange" and the rhetoric of "misery" to philosophic discourse, from mythos to logos?

The necessary, although inadequate, stage of philosophical transposition is the "transcendental" stage. We shall soon see why a reflection of this type does not satisfy the demands of philosophical anthropology, and to what extent its result remains deficient in comparison to the anticipatory comprehension of man that found its first expression in the *pathétique* of misery. But transcendental reflection itself will show its insufficiency.

The strength of "transcendental" reflection is twofold. First, it lies in the choice of a beginning: it looks for this beginning in an examination of the power of knowing. We may reprove as much as we like this reduction of man to a knowing being, but this heroic reduction is by no means the result of a prejudgment. It is the decision to situate all of man's characteristics with reference to the one that a critique of knowledge brings into focus. This leaves everything to be worked out subsequently; but all the questions, those concerned with doing and those with feeling, if they are preceded by an investigation of the power of knowing, are placed in a specific light that is suitable for a reflection on man. The fundamental categories of anthropology, including and above all those which characterize action and feeling, would not be anthropological categories if they did not first undergo the critical test of a "transcendental reflection," that is, an examination of the power of knowing.

In what way does this choice of a point of departure concern us? In that the first "disproportion" liable to philosophic investigation is the one which the power of knowing brings into view. What was previously "mélange" and "misery" for the pathetic understanding of man is now called "synthesis." In this way we shall rediscover, without worrying about critical orthodoxy, the grounds of the Kantian theory of the transcendental imagination, which is precisely a reflection on the "third term," on the "intermediate." This will therefore be our first stage on the road toward a transposition of the myths of mélange and the *pathétique* of misery into a philosophy of fallibility.

One might wonder how a reflection on the intermediary function of the imagination, in the Kantian sense, can concern a philosophy of fallibility. Here we find the second pre-eminence of a reflection of a "transcendental" style: it is a reflection that begins with the object or, to be more precise, with the *thing*. It is "upon" the *thing* that this reflection discerns the power of knowing, upon the thing that it discovers the specific disproportion of knowing, between receiving it and determining it. Upon the thing it apprehends the power of synthesis.

This meditation is transcendental and is a reflection because it starts from the *thing*. An immediate meditation on the non-coincidence of self with self is at once lost in the *pathétique*, and no introspection can give it the appearance of rigor. But reflection is not introspection; for reflection takes the roundabout way via the object; it is reflection *upon* the object. This is the way in which it is properly transcendental: it brings into view on the object that in the subject which makes the synthesis possible. This investigation of the conditions of possibility of an object's structure breaks with the *pathétique* and introduces the problem of disproportion and synthesis into the philosophic dimension. But the limitation of this reflection appears directly along with its strength: the synthesis that it reveals and inspects will be a synthesis only in the object, in the thing; a synthesis that is merely intentional, projected outside, into the world, into the structure of the objectivity it makes possible. Undoubtedly we will be able to call this power of synthesis "consciousness," as Kant did, and speak of the synthesis *as* "consciousness." This "consciousness," however, it not *for itself*; it remains purely intended, represented in a correlate. That is why another type of meditation will be necessary, so as to continue and pass from consciousness to self-consciousness.

FINITE PERSPECTIVE

The break introduced by reflection between sensibility and understanding is the point of departure of a transcendental study on man as intermediate and on the intermediate function of the imagination. As soon as reflection comes on the scene it sunders man, for reflection is essentially dividing, sundering. It is one thing, it says, to *receive* the presence of things, it is another to *determine* the meaning of things. To receive is to give oneself intuitively to their existence; to think is to dominate this presence in a discourse which discriminates by denomination and connects in articulate phrasing.

All progress in reflection is a progress in scission. We are going to devote ourselves first to this progression in scission, considering both parts of the divorce in succession.

It is upon the thing that I discover both the finitude of receiving and that kind of infinitude characteristic of determining, of saying, and intending which we shall see culminate in the verb.

One might think that a philosophic meditation on finitude could begin straightway by a study of *one's own body*. Indeed, every experience of finitude refers back to this unusual relation I have with my body. But this node of finitude is not what is first displayed: what is first displayed, what appears, are things, living beings, persons in the world. I am first directed toward the world. My finitude becomes a *problem* only when the belief that something really appears is shaken by dispute or contradiction. Then I shift my attention from *what* appears to him *to whom* it appears. But the shift from "the what" to "him to whom" does not yet inform me of my finitude. The first meaning I read in my body, insofar as the body is a mediation of appearance, is not that it is finite, but precisely that it is open onto. . . . It is this openness onto . . . which makes my body an originating mediator "*between*" myself and the world; it does not enclose me, like this bag of skin which, viewed from the outside, makes it seem like a thing in the midst of things. It opens me onto the world, either allowing perceived things to appear or making me dependent on things I lack and of which I experience the need and desire because they are elsewhere or even nowhere in the world. The body opens me onto the world even when it isolates me in suffering; for the solitude of suffering is still haunted by the threats of the world to which I feel myself exposed like an unprotected flank. It opens me to others insofar as it expresses, that is to say, displays the interior upon the exterior and becomes a sign for others, decipherable and offered to the reciprocity of consciousnesses. In a word, my body opens me to the world by everything it is able to do. It is implicated as a power in the instrumentality of the world, in the practicable aspects of this world that my action furrows through, in the products of work and art.

It is always *upon* the world and beginning from the manifestion of the world as perceived, threatening, and accessible that I apprehend the openness of my body, mediator of the intentional consciousness.

Shall I then say that my finitude consists in the world appearing to me *only* through the mediation of the body? This is true, and Kant was not wrong in identifying finitude and receptivity: according to him the finite is a rational being that does not create the objects of its representation but receives them. We might generalize this thesis and apply it to all other aspects of bodily mediation: to sustaining, lacking, expressing, being able. But what exactly is it that causes this bodily mediation to be finite? Is it not primarily the body's *openness* onto the world that is revealed in this marginal apperception which comes upon the body's mediation when the world appears to me? What I see first is not my bodily mediation but the world. Moreover, my bodily mediation shows at first not its finitude but its openness. In other words, the world is primarily not the boundary of my existence but its correlate: that is the meaning of the Refutation of Idealism in the *Critique of Pure Reason*.

What, then, makes this openness a *finite* one? The examination of *receptivity* will serve as a guide among the manifold modalities of bodily mediation. The reason for this choice lies in the fact that receptivity is the primary modality of this mediation; it is what makes things appear. The desirable, the fearful, the practicable, the useful, and all the aesthetic and moral predicates of the thing are secondary strata of primary appearing. Not that they are more "subjective" than the percept as such, but that they are "built upon" its primary foundation. Therefore it is necessary to begin with the percept.[1]

In what does the finitude of receiving consist? It consists in the perspectival limitation of perception. It causes every view of . . . to be a *point of view* on. . . . But this characteristic of the point of view, inherent in every viewing, is not directly noticed by me but realized reflectively. Thus it is *on* an aspect of the appearance, taken as an intentional correlate of receiving, that I must catch sight of the fini-

1. Percept: the object of perception as opposed to the perceiving or the subject of perception [Trans.].

tude of *my* point of view. This aspect of the appearance, which refers me back to my point of view, is the perceived object's insurmountable and invincible property of presenting itself from a certain angle, unilaterally. I never perceive more than one side at any given time, and the object is never more than the presumed unity of the flux of these silhouettes. Thus it is upon the object that I apprehend the perspectival nature of perception, which consists in the very inadequacy of the percept, that is, in the fundamental property that the sense outlined may always be *canceled* or *confirmed*, that it may reveal itself as *other* than the one I first presumed. The intentional analysis of this inadequacy makes me turn back from the object to myself as a finite center of perspective.

The presumed and precarious texture of sense impels me to break up, through reflection, the unity intended and outlined in a flow of silhouettes. Then the *same* object unravels into *other* profiles, into the "and then . . . and then" of the object's appearing.

The *otherness* of the silhouettes, which was discovered reflectively as watermarked within the identity of the object, makes me become aware of the unnoticed aspects of bodily mediation: my perceiving body is not only my openness onto the world, it is also the "here from where" the thing is seen. Let us examine more closely the moments of this regressive analysis which, from the otherness of the silhouettes, leads back to the perceiving body's character of origin and point of view. Let us first notice that by beginning with the object and not with the body, by moving from the percept to the perceiving, we do not risk being referred from the thing in the world to another thing in the world, which would be the body-object such as psychophysiology observes it from the outside and scientifically knows it. This body-object is still a percept. Indeed, it is the perceiving body that we are disengaging from the very characteristics of the percept. And it is necessary to disengage it by a special procedure because its function of mediation causes it to pass over itself and lose itself in the perceived term where the various operations of *perceiving* crash together, so to speak, and become identified with what is *perceived*.

Now, how can I observe that my body is the center of orientation, the zero origin, the "here from where" I see all that I can see? We must consider another intermediate stage between the *otherness* of silhouettes and the *here* of my body. This stage is that of the free mobility of my body: by changing my position I *can* make the object's aspect change; a certain behavior of my body commands the passivity of the perceived being. In this way my body proclaims itself as a condition of the changes of appearances. Kinesthetic sensations have the remarkable intentional property of designating my body as a motivating circumstance of the course of perception: *if* I turn my head, *if* I extend my hand, *if* I move about, *then* the thing appears in such and such a way. This flow of silhouettes is thus motivated by the flow of kinesthetic experience, it being understood that in direct consciousness the apperception of this kinesthetic flow loses itself in the apperception of the flow of silhouettes, and the latter in the appearance of the thing.

Here we have the ultimate reference: the otherness that my free mobility brings into play is an otherness in relation to an initial position that is always the absolute "here." The flow of silhouettes, to which the precariousness of perception referred me, in its turn refers me to the flow of my positions, and the latter to the origin of each position, the "here." It is to be noted that I am not speaking of the "here" of my hand or of my head, but only of the "here" of my body as an existing totality. In fact, only the displacements of my body as a totality denote a change of *place* and, thereby, the function of the place as a point of view. To account for this unique privilege of global movements to constitute the notion of point of view, even when this point of view is particularized by sight, hearing, or touch, we must add a further point to this analysis. When I break up the identity of the object into the otherness of its silhouettes, and these into the otherness of the active and passive positions of the body, I ascribe the diversity of the operations to the identity of a subject pole: these diverse silhouettes appear *to me*, that is, to this unity and to this identity of the subject pole which is, as it were, behind the diversity of the flow of silhouettes, behind the flow of positions. The "here from where" therefore concerns one's own body taken as one of the body's global positions on the ground of which the particular positions of the organs stand out. In this way my hand can change position without *my* having to change position. That is what Descartes meant when he said that the soul is united to the whole body. The soul moves about "somehow" *with* the body, which means that the self as an identical pole of all acts is where the body, taken as a whole, is.

Thus, the "it is I who," implied in all my intentional operations, makes the position of the body as a whole prevail in the constitution of the *here* over the position of its members. "Here" is the origin from which *I* see, not the origin from which my eye sees. Although the position of my eyes is the origin of the silhouettes seen, still it is not the position which constitutes the here, for my eye is I only by visual reference to what I see. Now the "I" of the "I see" is *here* only insofar as the body as a whole has a position from which it effectuates all its perceiving acts.

Thus, by a regressive route whose starting point was the characteristics of the percept, we have elucidated the finitude proper to receptivity. This peculiar finitude is identified with the notion of point of view or perspective. We see, then, in what sense it is true to say that the finitude of man consists in receiving his objects: in the sense that it belongs to the *essence* of perception to be inadequate, to the essence of this inadequacy to refer back to the onesided character of perception, and to the essence of the onesidedness of the thing's profiles to refer back to the otherness of the body's initial positions *from where* the thing appears. The fact that the *free* mobility of my body discloses this law of essence to me does not make the law unnecessary. It is precisely necessary that motor spontaneity originate from a zero origin. To perceive *from here* is the finitude of perceiving *something*. The point of view is the ineluctable initial narrowness of my openness to the world.

This necessity, however, is not a fate imposed from the *outside*. It only becomes so by a falsification that can easily be tracked down: I distinguish this narrowness from my very openness only by carrying it back, through a new regression beyond all my past "movements" to a first place that coincides with the event of my birth. I was born somewhere: from the moment I am "brought into the world" I perceive this world as a series of changes and re-establishments starting from this place which I did not choose and which I cannot find in my memory. My point of view then becomes detached from me like a fate that governs my life from the outside.

But the above regression is of an entirely different kind from the one which we performed starting from the percept. My birth is an event for others, not for myself. For others I was born in Valence; but I am here, and it is in relation to here that the others are there and elsewhere. My birth as an event for others assumes a position in relation to that "there" which for another is his "here": thus my birth does not belong to the primordial here, and I am not able to call up all my "heres" starting from my place of birth. On the contrary, beginning from the absolute here, which is the here and now— the *hic et nunc*—*I lose track* of my earliest "heres," and I borrow my place of birth from another's memory. This amounts to saying that my place of birth does not appear among the "heres" of my life and cannot therefore be their source.

Accordingly, at the end of this first analysis we shall maintain the following: Primal finitude consists in *perspective* or *point of view*. It affects our primary relation to the world, which is to "receive" objects and not to create them. It is not exactly synonymous with "receptivity" itself, which consists in our openness to the world. It is rather a principle of narrowness or, indeed, a closing within the openness. Neither is this finite openness synonymous with corporeity, which mediates our openness to the world. It consists more in the role of the body's zero origin, in the original "here" starting from which there are places in the world.

This relation between openness and perspective, a characteristic of the "receptivity" peculiar to perception, will be the melodic germ out of which we shall later be able to develop the other modalities of finitude.

INFINITE VERB

The very existence of a discourse on finitude should suffice to establish that the idea of perspective may be the most abstract of all the ideas about man and that it in no way attests the triumph of a concrete philosophy over the so-called abstract views of critical reflection. The very act of declaring man finite discloses a fundamental feature of this finitude: it is finite man *himself* who speaks of his *own* finitude. A statement on finitude testifies that this finitude knows itself and expresses itself. Thus it is of the nature of human finitude that it can experience itself only on the condition that there be a "view-on" finitude, a dominating look which has already begun to transgress[2] this finitude. In order for human finitude to be seen and expressed, a moment that surpasses it must be inherent in the situ-

2. Transgress and transgression, taken in their root meaning of stepping over or breaking through, and without their customary overtones, in English, of moral or legal violation [Trans.].

ation, condition, or state of being finite. This means that every description of finitude is abstract, i.e., separated and incomplete, if it
neglects to account for the transgression that makes discourse on
finitude possible. The complete discourse on finitude is a discourse
on the finitude and the infinitude of man.

In a sense it was Descartes, in his celebrated (and obscure) analysis of judgment, who first brought this relation of the finite and the
infinite to the center of philosophical anthropology. For all that man
is a power of judging, he is defined by a primordial disproportion.
But the distinction between a finite understanding and an infinite
will is not a good point of departure for us. First, this distinction
seems enclosed within the traditional framework of a faculty psychology; undoubtedly it has a sense outside of this tradition, and
later on we shall propose a reinterpretation of the Cartesian analysis.
But the finitude of the understanding is not the best approach to the
problem of the infinite. Moreover, the very use that Descartes makes
of the notions of finite and infinite prevents a satisfactory interpretation of the fourth *Meditation*. At first sight the opposition seems
purely quantitative: we know only a small number of things; on
the other hand, we hurry on to affirm many more things than we
know. This quantitative character of the understanding and the
will is, as it seems, confirmed by Descartes' reflections on the infinite increase of our knowledge—today we would say the progress
of "learning"—which he opposes to the existing infinite. Now, whoever speaks of increase brings in the concepts of more and less and
therefore number. The fourth *Meditation* goes in the same direction: "There is possibly an infinite number of things in the world of
which I have no idea in my understanding." By contrast, in the same
quantitative style, the will is said to have a limitless "extension,"
"capacity," or "amplitude." Taken literally, this distinction breaks
down under Spinoza's critique in the scholium to proposition 49 of
the second book of the *Ethics*.

How can we retain the driving force of the Cartesian distinction
between the finite and the infinite in man without going back to a
philosophy of the faculties, without assigning the finite to one faculty
and the infinite to another? The solution lies in taking the same point
of departure as in our reflection on the finite.

If finitude is primordially "point of view," the acts and operations
by which we become aware of point of view as point of view will re-

veal the most elementary connection between an *experience* of finitude and a *movement* transgressing this finitude.

Later on, the generalization of the notion of perspective will give us a progressively fuller view of that dialectic which Descartes formulated in the framework of a faculty psychology.

All perception is perspectival. But how could I recognize a perspective, in the very act of perceiving, if *in some way* I did not escape from my perspective?

In what way? Certainly by situating my perspective in relation to other possible perspectives that deny mine as the zero origin. But how can we avoid setting up this idea of non-perspective as a new point of view, which would be, as it were, an overview of the other points of view, a sweep over the centers of perspective? Finitude signifies that such a non-situated view or *Übersicht* does not exist. But if reflection upon point of view is not a point of view, then what is its nature?

The point of departure of our new analysis should not differ from the one that led us to the idea of perspective; it is *upon* the thing itself, we said, that I apprehend the perspectival character of perception, namely, *upon* the object's obvious property of always showing itself from only one side, then another. It is also upon the thing itself that I transgress my perspective. In point of fact, I can *express* this onesidedness only by *expressing* all the other sides that I do not currently see. The restrictive "only" stated in the proposition "each time I perceive *only* one side" comes to reflection only through a limiting act that replies to a limited situation. However, I do not come upon this limiting act directly, but reflectively as I apprehend the perspectivity of perception through reflection on the onesidedness of the perceived object. I anticipate the thing itself by relating the side which I see to those which I do not see but which I *know*. Thus I judge of the entire thing by going beyond its given side into the thing itself. This transgression is the intention to signify. Through it I bring myself before a sense which will never be perceived anywhere by anyone, which is not a superior point of view, which is not, in fact, a point of view at all but an inversion into the universal of all point of view.

If I now note that to signify is to intend, the transgression of the point of view is nothing else than speech as the possibility of expressing, and of expressing the point of view itself. Therefore, I am not merely a situated onlooker, but a being who intends and expresses as an intentional transgression of the situation. As soon as I speak, I speak of things in their absence and in terms of their non-perceived sides. Thus the finite perspectival intention that gives me the perceived presence in the living present, which is the present of the presence, is never alone and bare. Insofar as this perspectival intention is saturated with presence it is always enmeshed in a more or less complete relationship of fulfillment with respect to another aim which penetrates it through and through, which literally passes right through it, and to which speech is originally linked. This aim is the intention behind speaking. In being born I enter into the world of language that precedes me and envelops me. The mute look is caught up in speech that articulates the sense of it. And this ability to express sense is a continual transcendence, at least in intention, of the perspectival aspect of the perceived here and now.

This dialectic of signifying and perceiving, of saying and seeing, indeed seems absolutely primal, and the project of a phenomenology of perception, wherein the moment of saying is postponed and the reciprocity of saying and seeing destroyed, is ultimately untenable. On this score the first of Husserl's *Logical Investigations* and the first chapters of Hegel's *Phenomenology of Spirit* concur.

Expression, in the sense of verbal expression (*Ausdruck*), according to the first of the *Logical Investigations*, is a significative indication in the sense that it announces to others what I mean. It conveys meaning to others, however, only because it signifies, that is, denotes a sense, a represented content. The announcement, the communication to others, is possible only through designation, i.e., the proper significance of language.[3] Now, through its signifying function, language conveys not my perception's finite perspective but the sense that intentionally transgresses my perspective. Language transmits the intention, not the perception of what is seen. Everyone to whom this sense is conveyed "fulfills" it in varying degrees in perception, "in the flesh," but from some particular point of view; or else they fulfill it only in imagination, or perhaps not at all. To achieve meaning is not to bestow it directly; the word has the ad-

---

3. In the same sense Plato distinguishes the twofold function of λόγος: it communicates to others (it indicates) and it designates something (it signifies). Likewise, in Aristotle's *On Interpretation* "the interpretation" of the πάθη (affects) of the soul is the statement, which for Husserl is indication.

mirable property of making its sonority transparent, of fading away bodily in giving rise to the act that confers the sense. In short, the word becomes a sign.

In the sign dwells the transcendence of the λόγος of man: from the very first word I designate the self-identity of the signified, the meaning-unity which another discourse of mine will be able to re-capture and which the discourse of another person will be able to catch hold of in flight and return to me in a dialogue. However great "misunderstandings" might be, they dramatize an "entente" which has always been in progress, which no man inaugurates, and which everyone has been continuing since man first began to speak. What is said, the λεκτόν of my λέγειν, the *dictum* of every *dictio*, transcends, as an ideal meaning-unity, the simple experience of the statement.

This transcendence of *saying* is attested by its excess in relation to its fulfillment. Without being paradoxical we may say that the least fulfilled expressions are the most instructive in this connection, and that the height of signification is that of the one that in principle cannot be fulfilled, the absurd signification.[4] I am a power of absurd significations. This single power attests that I do not exhaust my-self in an intentionality of fulfilled presence, but that I am a two-fold intentionality: on the one hand, an intentionality signifying emptily, a power to speak in the absence of the this-here; on the other, a fulfilled intentionality, an openness to receiving, and a power of seeing in the presence of the this-here.

But by its nature of being impossible to fulfill, the absurd significa-tion only reveals the property that all meaning has of exceeding every present perceptive fulfillment: I say more than I see when I signify.

It may be objected that what I know in the case of the perceived thing is the condensed and sedimented result of the thing's per-ceptibility, and that this perceptibility is the symbolic reference of the seen side to the unseen side, of one sensory register to another, of color to sound and to taste, in an infinite chain of correspondences. But in order for this play of correspondences and references to be

4. There is a progression from the expressions which do not co-signify or connote anything, and remain, as it were, in suspension, to those which can-not be fulfilled because the fulfillment cancels itself by incompatible intuitions (square circle), to those expressions which are grammatically impossible ("green is therefore," wherein the conjunction has the impossible pretension of being an attribute).

possible, by which one appearance anticipates all the others, in order for *the* thing to regulate this symbolism inside one and the same sensory register and from one sensory register to another, it is necessary for language to come to the aid of the body, to become the organ of this mutual reinforcement of the various senses and to place in a *name* the rule of this reinforcement and mutual reference of appearances.

The act of "denomination," for instance "tree," in signifying the constancy of a central pole of the thing's appearance, transcends all the appearances at the same time as it is verified in the play of correspondences by which one appearance designates another: the green by the sappy odor, the sappy odor by the rustling, etc. Because the name signifies, I *can say* that one appearance signifies all the others. Language, insofar as it penetrates all the sensory appearances of the thing, causes perception to be significative. Surely if the body were not the organic root of all intersensory reinforcements, verification would not be possible: but it is one thing to make fulfillment possible in a coherent sequence of perceptions, and another to put forth a meaning-unity to be verified in a stream of perceptions. Certainly the body as the bearer of the various senses (sight, touch, hearing) is the ground for the transposition and the mutual reinforcement of appearances; but this unity of the body is merely the *perspectival* unity that regulates the orderly fulfillment of signification. We need the "name" to give a ground to the meaning-unity, the non-perspectival unity of the thing, the one which is announced to and understood by another and which he will verify in his turn and from his position in a sequence of converging perceptions. In effecting this process of verification, his body will provide a *different* perspective, a *different* structuration of the mutual signification of colors through sounds and smells. But it is the same expressed signification that will be verified in a *different* perspective.

The dialectic of "name" and "perspective," therefore, is the very dialectic of infinitude and finitude.

The same analysis, set forth in the language of the Husserlian *phenomenology*, may be recast and completed in the language of Hegel's *Phenomenology of Spirit*. We are never only in the certainty of the this-here-now for this particular self. We are always already in the dimension of truth. From our first certainty, the one that comes of our being set among the things of the world, we speak universal truth. The equivalence of certainty and truth is what we pursue through consciousness. It is on account of this task that the *Phenomenology* is oriented such that it has "its own end as a goal at the outset." The fact that the self is *at variance* with itself is the indefeasible worm in the fruit of the immediate; and this difference is already present in the "of" that renders the expression "knowledge *of* the immediate" dialectical. The "of" that draws attention to the intentionality of consciousness conceals the dialectic of certainty and truth. Now, in Hegel, as in Husserl, language introduces this dialectic: "We do not actually and absolutely say what in this sense-certainty we really *mean*." As soon as we put the "now is the night" into the body of speech a new now appears "but as what is not night." The now, spoken and preserved in speech, has become a "not-this," a "not-now." The universal is born in this denial which the flux of appearances opposes to the permanence of our words. "Language, however, as we see, is the more truthful; in it we ourselves refute directly and at once our own 'meaning' [*Meinung*]; and since universality is the real truth of sense-certainty, and language merely expresses *this* truth, then it is not possible at all for us even to express in words any sensuous existence which we 'mean.' "[5]

Thus the gap between certainty and truth is irreducible. It is witnessed in the difference between the fullness of the least look and the poverty of the simplest truth in which it is expressed: "It is," says Parmenides' *Poem*. "What a lot of water," says the President[6] who is "amazed" by the flood, the sight of which submerges speech.[7]

5. Hegel, *The Phenomenology of Mind*, trans. J. B. Baillie (New York: Macmillan, 1961), pp. 151–52 [Trans.]

6. *"Que d'eau, que d'eau"*—attributed to Marshal MacMahon, second President of the Third French Republic, 1873–1879, upon inspecting a floodsite [Trans.].

7. It will be said that this analysis proves just the opposite of the preceding one; Husserl's empty signification will never be adequately fulfilled by intuition: empty signification is therefore the richest; Hegel's initial certainty is not taken in by truth: truth, therefore, is the poorer of the two. A quite evident contrast, and one that is very illuminating. In a sense, certainty is the weaker in universality because it is perspectival. This is why meaning transcends it as a valid unity; but certainty is the richer in presence because it is open onto the world. That is why meaning overtakes it only by multiplying the mediations until abstraction, by means of its peculiar multiplication, is equal to the supreme concretion of actual Reality.

What the two analyses have in common is the following: (1) the initial

This transcendence of signification over perception, of speaking over perspective, is what makes the reflection on point of view as such possible: I am not immersed in the world to such an extent that I lose the aloofness of signifying, of intending, aloofness that is the principle of speech. In asserting this aloofness, which does not set up any superior point of view but aims at the truth without point of view, I convert my "here" from an absolute placement into an any-place-whatever, which is relative to all the others, in a geo-metrical and social space in which there is no privileged emplace-ment. I know that I am here because I am not merely the zero point, but I reflect on it; and I know at the same time that the presence of things is given to me from a point of view, because I intended the thing in its meaning that is beyond all point of view.

But this transcendence of signification, witnessed by the gap be-tween the truth-intention and present certainty, has not yet revealed the *infinite* moment of speech. There is a great, if not immediately apparent, truth in the Cartesian thesis of the finitude of the under-standing and the infinitude of the will, both of which are implied in the power of judging. Descartes prompts us to proceed to a second reduction after the one that showed the polarity of speech and per-spective, signification and perception. This second reduction, within what we called as a whole the sense of signification, intention, and speech, ought to bring out the moment of affirmation.[8]

Here again we must not move too quickly to the side of the sub-ject, act or noesis, but proceed reflectively beginning with the object, content and noema.

Up to now we have pretended to ignore that the authentic "signifi-

---

disproportion of signifying and seeing, of truth and certainty; (2) the identi-fication of the transcendence of signifying and truth with speech, with λόγος; (3) the value of negativity that is attached to this transcendence: *void* of sig-nification, the not-this, the not-this-here of the universal. I am not concerned here with that negative accent of the universal's transcendence; we will return to that when we consider the negative aspects of finitude, privation, and fault.

8. The first reduction in Descartes shows the inspection of the mind to be superior to perception (second *Meditation*). It leads to the "idea" of the third *Meditation*. The second reduction is the one that brings about the disjunction of the understanding and the will: "For by the understanding alone I neither affirm nor deny anything, but apprehend (*percipio*) the ideas of things that I can affirm or deny" (fourth *Meditation*).

cant speech," as Aristotle calls it in the treatise *On Interpretation*, is
the composite discourse which he calls λόγος (§ 4), the phrasing of
the world or judgment. Aristotle here avails himself of Plato's discovery in the *Cratylus*, the *Theaetetus*, and the *Sophist*, where for the
first time the distinction between noun and verb is given its profound
significance and set down as the cornerstone of human discourse. Indeed, our whole meditation on the transcendence of speech over perspective leads to a reflection on the verb. Why put such stock in the
significance of the verb?

Let us start with the analysis of the verb in the treatise *On Interpretation* (§3). The verb, Aristotle says, is a noun-meaning shot
through with an added meaning (προσσημαίνει) and even by a twofold supra-signification. On the one hand, the verb designates the
tense, i.e., it puts the verb's nominal meaning into present existence;
to say that "Socrates is walking" is to posit the present existence of
the walking, and all the other tenses are only inflections of the present. This positing of existence affects the whole nominal meaning of
the verb, that is, the whole bloc which complements the subject and
which will eventually be split up into copula and predicate: in "Socrates is sitting," the verb is the bloc "is sitting," and it is this unity
that supra-signifies (*consignificat*, St. Thomas says) the tense. On
the other hand, besides this assertion of existence, the verb adds to
the noun-meaning that it already has the attribution to the subject;
what it says is said "with reference to something else." This second
function does not reside in another part of speech, as if, e.g., the
present existence were designated by the copula and the attribution
by the predicate: it is the whole verb bloc that assumes the two functions. "Socrates is walking" means that the walk "exists now" and
that the walk is "*said of*" Socrates.

In the verb's twofold intention the human sentence finds at once
its unity of signification and its capacity for truth and error. The verb
is what makes the sentence "hold together" since it ascribes the attributed signification to the subject of attribution by means of its
supplemental signification. By asserting being, it introduces the human sentence into the ambiguous realm of the true and the false.

Aristotle's admirable analysis sets us on the threshold of the decisive reflection. Indeed, the soul of the verb is affirmation, the saying
of *yes* or *no*. By means of the verb we may affirm or deny something of

something.[9] Now, with affirmation and negation appears the transcendence, no longer merely of signification in general over perception, but of speech, taken as verb, over its own signified contents taken as nouns. Aristotle had already clarified this fundamental "possibility" of making, with the same noun-meanings, not merely an affirmation and a negation, but (and he lists them in the following order, which is very important) a false negation, a false affirmation, a true affirmation, and a true negation.[10] A bit earlier we were considering absurd significations; now we must consider the verb's power of multiplying the primary significations of "nouns," first by negations and then by false negations. The possibility of the *false negation*, which Aristotle puts at the head of his list, is the symbol of the transcendence of the "verb" over the ordinary signification, over the "noun" as a signified, established, and sedimented signification.

Aristotle did not consider the *power* or potency to judge revealed by the verb. What interested him in that "possibility" of denying everything one has affirmed and of affirming everything one has denied is not the terrible and admirable "power" of human affirmation, but the very opposition of affirmation and negation with regard to the same attribute ascribed to the same subject. In short, it was the approach to the logic of contradiction.

Now, following the tradition leading from St. Thomas to Descartes, and Malebranche, it is up to us to reflect on this fourfold power of the verb and to rediscover therein the *electio*, the *liberum arbitrium*, which may also be termed *liberum judicium*, the power of contraries, the power to affirm or deny. In short, it is what that tradition called "volition" in judgment.[11] It is in relation to this positive

9. "We mean by affirmation a statement ascribing one thing to another; we mean by negation a statement denying one thing of another" (*On Interpretation* § 6).

10. Ibid. § 6.

11. Aristotle also started this analysis in the *Nicomachean Ethics*, III, with his study of the voluntary and the involuntary aspects in actions, of deliberation and preference in the choice of means. But this theory of practical judgment remains confined to ethics and has no relation to the study of the verb conducted in other respects in the framework of the *Organon*. To bring these two lines of analysis together, in my opinion, is to show the noetico-noematic correlation between the power of affirming (noesis) and the supra-signification of the verb (noema).

power of affirming that the primary significations of nouns are, in a sense, passions of the soul, that our conceptions are passively received. Their sense is received, but they are posited by belief: to believe is to affirm and to affirm is "to do." In this way we see man's control over his thoughts and his responsibility or the "merit of praise or blame," as Descartes says in the *Principles*. For even when the will "follows" the light of the understanding, it is still independent in its decision to *pay attention*, consider, and apply itself to this light.

In this way the Cartesian dialectic of the understanding and the will, whose literal interpretation we had to reject, is restored to us. Descartes himself points the way to a second reading of the fourth *Meditation* wherein the purely quantitative sense of the finite and the infinite would be superseded. When Gassendi objected that the understanding has at least as much extension as the will, since the latter could not be applied to a thing of which we have no idea, Descartes replied: "So while I confess that there is nothing that we will, about which we do not understand something, I deny that our understanding and our will are equally extended; for we may have several volitions about the same thing of which we can understand only very little."[12]

"To have several volitions about the same thing." Descartes thus rediscovers an affirmation that is at the core of Aristotle's treatise *On Interpretation*: with the same subjects and attributes it is possible to affirm and deny, or, what is more, to affirm and deny the presence of what is absent and to affirm and deny the presence of what is present.

Now, this mutiple volition about the same things goes beyond the finitude of the understanding. The extension, the vastness of the will is thus its independence, and this independence is an indivisible quality. When the understanding presents no clear ideas for the subject to choose among, this independence takes the form of indifference. But failing indifference, this independence is still absence of constraint, and even, in a certain sense, a power to do or not to do, to affirm or to deny, to follow or to flee, and therefore a power of contraries. The letters to Mesland show in what sense the will conserves, failing all indifference, i.e., complete equivalence in motives and reasons, "this positive power we have of pursuing the worse al-

12. Descartes, *Replies to Objections* V.

though we know the better." The "present" character of intuition, weakness and proneness to fatigue, the inconstancy of our attention[13] constitute sufficient argument that there is still merit in fixing one's attention on the true and that evidence itself is an action. "All that occurs or happens anew is generally called by the philosophers a passion insofar as the subject to which it occurs is concerned, and an action in respect of him who causes it to occur."[14] The distinction between the will and the understanding in the fourth *Meditation* was only a particular instance of the distinction between the actions and passions of the soul,[15] in the sense that to affirm and to choose are actions of the soul whereas our perceptions or cognitions "are found in us, because it is often not our soul which makes them what they are, and because it always receives them from the things which are represented by it."[16] Thus the dialectic of the Infinite and the Finite comes into play between *Doing* and *Receiving*.

The Cartesian analysis thus leads us back to that power of affirmation that the treatise *On Interpretation* taught us to ascribe to the *verb* and which St. Thomas and Descartes teach us to find in the volitional moment of affirmation. All our analyses therefore lead to the identity of the verb and assent, consent, election (or whatever one may want to call it). If we adopt the Husserlian language and the noesis–noema correlation, we may say that the supra-signification of the verb is the correlative noema of the noesis which we now see to be constituted by the volitional moment of affirmation.

This correlation of assent and the verb keeps us clear of many mistakes; we will consider only two of them closely related to our own analysis. The first concerns the use we made of Descartes and the reinterpretation that enabled us not to reject him. Now, the danger in the Cartesian analysis lies not only in interpreting the distinction between the finite and the infinite in quantitative terms,

13. We see here that the finitude of the understanding consists less in a quantitative narrowness than in the necessity of thinking successively, in the merely present character of intuition, in the fatigue of attention: to P. Mesland, May 2, 1644. Likewise, the end of the fourth *Meditation*: "I notice a certain weakness in my nature in that I cannot continually concentrate my mind on one single thing." The end of the sixth *Meditation* compares fatigue and the instantaneity of intuition. Cf. also *Principles*, I, 13.

14. Descartes, *The Passions of the Soul*, I, 2.

15. Ibid., I, 17.

16. Ibid.

but in separating human infinitude from the demand for truth. Truth, it seems, lies with the idea, but only our assent is free. To be sure, Descartes never stopped repeating that the greater the light in the understanding, the greater the inclination in the will, and that the freedom of indifference is the lowest degree of freedom. But that does not disarm the distinction that puts the will, freedom, and the infinite on one side, and the understanding, truth, and the finite on the other. All the dangers of voluntarism are inscribed in this dichotomy.

Now, if we link the subjective and volitional moment of affirmation to the objective moment of the *verb* that is significative by itself, there is no longer any distinction between two faculties or between an infinite will and a finite understanding. The correlation of affirmation and the verb, i.e., the correlation of an act and a signification, or better yet of a "supra-signification," is, if one sticks to this language, the correlation of the will and the understanding. The will no longer has any privilege of infinity that does not likewise belong to the understanding. That is why it is better to abandon this faculty psychology altogether and substitute for it a theory of signification that (1) takes into account the radical distinction of nouns and verbs, and (2) links the volitional moment of affirmation to the proper signification of the verb.

Such a discord, however, can be found in our own text: we first situated man's transcendence over his situation or perspective in speech *qua* significance. Meaning, we said, is the non-point of view. Thus the truth-intention, interpreted first in Husserlian terms and then in Hegelian terms, appeared to constitute the moment of man's infinitude. Then signification was split into the noun and the verb. The transcendence of speech centered upon the verb, and the verb revealed its soul of affirmation. In moving the accent from signification in general (which was understood rather in the sense of "noun") onto the verb, we move it also from the truth-intention to the freedom-intention.

Here again the correlation between assent and a specific moment of speech prevents the separation of the two problematics of truth and freedom. The verb supra-signifies: that means that it signifies primarily as a noun and is built on the primary intention of signifying. Thereby our freedom of affirming—insofar as it is tied to the verb— is rooted in the soil of noun-meanings. Moreover, by means of the twofold character of supra-signification—reference to present time and predicative relation turned toward a subject of the verb—the verb binds human affirmation to the truth-intention in a twofold way. The verb considered as a declaration of being is the reference to the present time, and the reference to the subject is the verb as relational. The two dimensions of truth, existential and relational, are thus implied in the verb. Accordingly, if freedom of judgment lies in the act of affirmation, if the intentional correlate of affirmation is the verb, and if the verb aims at the truth, then freedom and truth form the noesis–noema pair that is constitutive of human affirmation.

PURE IMAGINATION

Our reflection on the thing has given us an initial result: in discovering the breach between the finite and the infinite, it has also uncovered the "disproportion" between the verb that gives expression to being and truth at the risk of falling into error, and, on the other hand, the passive look that is riveted to appearance and perspective. This "disproportion" is at once the duality of the understanding and sensibility, in Kantian terms, and the duality of the will and the understanding in Cartesian language.

This discovery of "disproportion" gives rise to the problem of the third term, the intermediate term, which we shall call pure imagination for reasons that will soon become evident. Now, the surprising thing is that this third term is not susceptible of being captured in itself, as were the notion of sense in the consciousness of perspective and the verb in the consciousness of signification, then in the consciousness of affirmation. The surprising thing is that this third term is not given in itself but only in the thing. In other words, for a merely transcendental reflection, man effects his own synthesis only in intention. Or, in still other words, if we can speak of the consciousness of synthesis or of the synthesis as consciousness, this consciousness is not yet self-consciousness, not yet "man."

What is the thing? It is the unity that is already realized in a correlate of speech and point of view; it is the synthesis as effected outside. That synthesis, inasmuch as it is in a correlate, bears the name of objectivity. Indeed, objectivity is nothing other than the indivisible unity of an appearance and an ability to express; the thing shows itself *and* can be expressed. An appearance which could in no way be expressed, which would exclude itself from the realm of discourse, and which would not allow itself to be anticipated in any "sense" would literally be the fleeting appearance that Plato compares to the statues of Daedalus, which nothing can tie down. The unbound appearance is as nothing. But conversely, I bind nothing other than that which shows itself; speech is the determination of the appearance. That is so true that the synthesis *of* the thing and *on* the thing is what enabled reflection to distinguish the inadequacy of perception, what we might call the disconnectedness of silhouettes, and, on the other hand, the transcendence of sense over that flow of silhouettes, and finally, that of the verb over the purely nominal sense. It is the thing that points to man as point of view and as speech.

We could not emphasize this point too much. The objectivity of the object is by no means "in" consciousness; it stands over against it as that to which it relates. It is in this quality that objectivity can serve as a clue or a transcendental guide in the very consciousness that the pure ego acquires of this synthesis. Consequently, objectivity in no way prejudges the real unity of man for himself, for this synthesis is first intentional. Consciousness makes itself an intermediary primarily by projecting itself into the thing's mode of being. It becomes a mean between the infinite and the finite by delineating the ontological dimension of things, namely, that they are a synthesis of meaning and presence: here consciousness is nothing else than that which stipulates that a thing is a thing only if it is in accordance with this synthetic constitution, if it can appear *and* be expressed, if it can affect me in my finitude *and* lend itself to the discourse of any rational being. Consequently, in order to stress that the objectivity of the object is constituted on the object itself, I prefer to say that the synthesis is primarily one of meaning and appearance rather than a synthesis of the intelligible and the sensible. The point where I differ from Kant is clear: the real *a priori* synthesis is not the one that is set forth in the "principles," i.e., in the judgments that would be prior to all the empirical propositions of the physical domain. Kant reduced the scope of his discovery to the restricted dimensions of an epistemology. The objectivity of the object is reduced to the scientific aspect of objects belonging to a domain carved out by the history of the sciences. But criticism is more than epistemology, transcendental reflection is more than an exploration of the scientific nature of the objects of science. The real *a priori* synthesis does not appear even in the first principles; it consists in the thing's objectival character (rather than objective, if objective means scientific), namely that property of being thrown before me, at once given to my point of view *and* capable of being communicated, in a language comprehensible by any rational being. The objectivity of the object consists in a certain expressibility adhering to the appearance of anything whatsoever.[17]

This objectivity is neither in consciousness nor in the principles of science; it is rather the thing's mode of being. It is the ontological mode of those "beings" which we call things. Heidegger—whom we shall eventually refuse to follow—is right in saying that the Copernican revolution is first of all the return from the ontic to the ontological, i.e., from the "thing" considered as a "being"[18] among "beings" ("there are" things as "there are" men as "there are" gods) to its ontological constitution. Objectivity indicates this synthetic constitution itself as a uniting of meaning to presence. In order for something to be an object, it must conform to this synthetic constitution: "Ontic truth conforms necessarily to ontological truth. There again is the legitimate interpretation of the meaning of the 'Copernican revolution.' "[19]

Let us go back now, by a further step in reflection, to the function which makes this synthesis *on* the thing possible, which makes it possible by projecting in advance the objectivity of the object, i.e., the mode of being proper to it and in virtue of which it can appear and be expressed.

This reflection is transcendental and not psychological because

17. An excellent example of objectival synthesis, which outruns the properly epistemological setting of the Kantian notion of objectivity, is provided by Kant himself in his examination of the categories of quality. Quality, he observes, allows itself to be determined in "an anticipation of the perception" according to which no perception can be constituted without a *degree* in the quality; by means of the "degree" every quality is expressible, i.e., capable of being distinguished, recognized, stated. Thus, cherry red affects me, but in such a way that it makes possible *a priori* the ever more subtle discernment of a connoisseur. The quality is such that it can at once be felt and determined. That is its objectival character.

18. The French *l'étant* renders Heidegger's *das Seiende*, which we render "being." Other translations include "essents," "entity," "existent," "thing-in-being," etc. [Trans.].

19. Heidegger, *Kant and the Problem of Metaphysics*.

·the thing's ontological constitution, its objectivity, serves as a guide to the coming to awareness of the subjective synthesis itself: the secret of the synthesis of the finite and the infinite in "the soul" consists in the *reference of* this "soul" to the objectival synthesis, at least at this stage of our reflection which is voluntarily theoretical and strictly transcendental. Accordingly, I shall say that I myself become a synthesis of speech and perspective in this projection of objectivity. But what does that mean?

The elucidation of an image that we have used several times, the image of openness, will serve as a transition to the Kantian idea of pure imagination. At the beginning of our investigation of the idea of perspective, we said that our body was primordially—that is, before we noted its perspectival function—an *opening onto* the world. We were able to constitute the notion of perspective only as a kind of narrowness of our openness. Of course, this image is borrowed from the description of looking as were those of point of view, field, form, and horizon. But this image has the virtue of suggesting something like a mixture of point of view and meaning; for if point of view is a characteristic of openness, namely its narrowness, openness indicates that my point of view is transgressed, that I am not enclosed within each silhouette, but that I have access to a space of expressibility through the very appearance of the thing under its successive aspects.

Perspective and transgression were thus the two poles of a single function of openness. The image of openness, then, already indicated the "mixture" of sensory affection and intellectual determination that we are now trying to realize.

The image of openness calls up another image: that of clarity or light as it is found in the Platonic and Cartesian tradition. What is noteworthy in this image is that it suggests the idea of a medium in which one sees; we do not see the light but in the light. Light is thus the space of appearance, but light is also a space of intelligibility. Light, as openness, is a medium of appearance and expressibility.

In this way we have reconstituted, by the roundabout way of analogy, the presuppositions of the Kantian problem of pure imagination—and we shall soon know why the essential was discovered indirectly by way of image and not directly by way of immediate reflection.

It is not by chance that our anthropology of the finite and the infinite encounters Kant at this stage of its development. Every philosophy that holds both that the receptivity of perception is irreducible to discourse and system and that determining thought is irreducible to receptivity, in short, every philosophy that refuses both absolute idealism and radical empiricism, rediscovers for itself the Kantian problem of the synthesis of the rules of expressibility (or the "categories") and the conditions of appearance (or "pure intuition") in the "transcendental imagination." Therefore, let us travel for a while with Kant.

If to judge is to subsume an intuition under a concept, "there must be some third term, which is homogeneous on the one hand with the category, and on the other hand with the appearance, and which thus makes the application of the former to the latter possible. This mediating representation must be pure, that is, void of all empirical content, and yet at the same time, while it must in one respect be *intellectual*, it must in another be *sensible*. Such a representation is the transcendental schema."[20]

What interests us in the theory of the transcendental imagination is that this third term does not exist *for itself*: it completely exhausts itself in the act of constituting objectivity; for itself the imaginative synthesis is *obscure*. The schematism is "an art concealed in the depths of the human soul, whose real modes of activity nature is hardly likely ever to allow us to discover, and to have open to our gaze."[21] It would be a mistake to reduce Kant's declaration to a confession of the failure of a philosophy that starts from the duality of understanding and sensibility. It is the profound discovery that this duality is overcome somewhere, in the object, but that this unity is not susceptible of being fully reflected: whereas the objectivity of the object is what is clearest and most manifest—it is the true *lumen naturale*—the transcendental imagination for which it is the correlate remains an enigma. It remains an enigma because we understand what receiving and being affected mean; we understand what it means to determine intellectually; we understand that these two powers cannot exchange their functions—"The understanding can intuit nothing, the senses can think nothing." It is because we under-

20. Kant, *Critique of Pure Reason*, A138, trans. N. Kemp Smith (New York: St. Martin's Press, 1961), p. 181 (with minor change in translation) [Trans.].

21. Ibid., A141, p. 183 [Trans.].

stand all this that their common root is "unknown to us" and that the
movement from the clear, objectival synthesis to the obscure "intermediary" is "forever arduous." Thus there is, as it were, a blind point
at the center of the luminous vision, which is that function of the soul
which Kant says is "blind but indispensable." In short, this mediating term has no intelligibility of its own.

It is true that Kant pushes the regression further toward the middle term, the vehicle of the synthesis, and goes back to time, or, as
he says, to the "transcendental determination of time" in order to
solve the enigma of the "third term." Is not time the mixture *par excellence*? Is not time the condition of all lived diversity, and, to deal
freely with the Kantian idea of diversity, the condition of every surprise, of every encounter, of all incoherence, of every innovation,
appearance, and excision? In short, is not time essentially distended,
and is not this disconnectedness what makes time "homogeneous
with the phenomenon," to speak again in Kantian terms? And furthermore, is not time *determinable* in the highest degree by the understanding since all the categories are rooted in the understanding
in the form of schemata? And indeed, what is truly brilliant in the
theory of the schematization is that, in determining time, each category makes itself intuitive and receives a dimension full of imagery.
In adding unit to unit I determine time as a "series." Kant himself
says: "I generate time itself in the apprehension of the intuition."
Now, in determining time I have also generated number, "a representation which comprises the successive addition of homogeneous
units." By the same stroke I have given a schema to the pure category of quantity. The same time, which a bit earlier had the aspect
of disconnectedness, is now, considered as a series, the pure image
of all magnitudes. Time is therefore that mediating order, homogeneous both with the sensible whose very style of dispersion and distention it is, and with the intelligible for which it is the condition of
intuition since it lends itself to that intelligible determination that we
call "series." The marvel of time is the coincidence of "manifold"
and "series."

We can add to that marvel, for time is determinable in terms of
still other relations: it is also that which can be filled or empty; in
this way it is homogeneous with the categories of quality, each sensation having a "degree" according to the measure in which it "fills"
a given time. Or I can consider time as an order in which something

either persists in time, follows after something else in time, or in which two things exist in one and the same time by a reciprocal action: the order of time or time as an order therefore provides the relational categories with the helpful schemata of permanence in time, oriented causality and reciprocal causality.

Have we not, as Heidegger says, gained access, thanks to time, to the "original phenomenological knowledge of the inner and unified structure of transcendence"?[22]

Strictly speaking, we have only sharpened the paradox by a more subtle approximation. We still state a duality when we say that time is both the form of all diversity *and* that it allows itself to be determined by the understanding and its categories, that it scatters and orders, that it diversifies and unifies. Did St. Augustine not say that it was *distentio* and *intentio*? To say that time is the unity of that duality is to name the difficulty as well as to situate it—which is not nothing—but it does not solve it. For the third term to be intelligible in itself we would have to show that it is the "common root" of understanding and sensibility. Now, such a radical genesis of the concepts of understanding and intuition beginning with the transcendental determination of time—thus a genesis of the categories from the schemata—remains a pious wish. Time lets itself be determined only in these several ways—time-series, time-content, time-order, scope of time—because relations that are pure and purely intellectual determine it. No one has ever shown how, from the consideration of time alone, one can educe a well-formulated notional order. We simply void the problem when, with Heidegger, we speak of the transcendence of finitude. A question such as "How can man, finite and as such consigned to being and destined to the reception of it, how can he, before any reception, know being, that is, intuit it without however being its creator?" is a truncated question. To know being is not merely to let it appear but also to determine it intellectually, to order it, to express it. That is why a philosophy of finitude, even interpreted as transcending finitude, is not sufficient to the problem. A philosophy of synthesis—the synthesis of finitude and rationality—is required. The substitution was only possible at the price of the reduction of the problem of objectivity to that of letting-appear; the tension has been eliminated from the problem in eliminating the

22. Heidegger, *Kant and the Problem of Metaphysics.*

pole of the understanding in favor of the pole of intuition. The specific problem of the coincidence of rationality and intuition, of thinking and seeing, in objectivity, has been eliminated. If we are to do justice to the dramatic aspect of the object, we can no longer be satisfied with formulas that merely christen the difficulty when they do not hide it: openness, transcendence, letting the object interpose, etc. are deceptive expressions because they conceal the essential, i.e., that a notional order applies to what appears to intuition. Because Kant was concerned about such an order, about such a discursiveness demanded by the very expressibility of the object, he could not be satisfied with a vague, formless transcendence that would be a simple field of appearances but by no means an intelligible order. Consequently, he could not draw this order from time itself, but, on the contrary, had to determine time by the category. We cannot understand the problem by throwing out what constitutes the essence of rationality, namely, an articulate discourse. That is why in Kant the schemata remain an *application* of the categories to the phenomena, and could not be considered as their radical origin. There is not even any reason here to distinguish between the first and the second editions of the *Critique of Pure Reason*. For it is the first edition that states: "Upon the categories is based all formal unity in the synthesis of imagination,"[23] and "the schema is simply the pure synthesis, determined by a rule of that unity, in accordance with concepts, to which the category gives expression."[24] Moreover, in thus endowing them with an image by means of the representation of a general process of the imagination, the schema restricts the category's range of meaning. Kant had always been aware that there was less in the schema than in the category: the outline of a triadic genesis of pure concepts (B110–111)—unity, plurality, totality / reality, negation, limitation / subsistence, causality, community / existence, possibility, necessity—is the sign that a radical genesis of pure concepts is rather to be looked for in a purely notional dialectic ruled by a "separate act of the understanding."[25] But Kant did not explore this path.

If, then, we respect the initial polarity that generates the prob-

23. *Critique of Pure Reason*, A125 (Kemp Smith), p. 147 (with minor change in translation) [Trans.].

24. Ibid., A142, p. 183 (translation changed) [Trans.].

25. Ibid., A111, p. 117 [Trans.].

lem itself, the enigma of the transcendental imagination remains in-
tact. We can designate it only by a twofold requisite: going from
the top down we shall say that thought, a power for determining and
expressing, must needs apply itself to appearances; in Kantian terms:
the unity of apperception "presupposes or includes a synthesis"
(A118). We shall even go so far as to say that the "principle of the
necessary unity of pure (productive) synthesis of imagination, prior
to apperception, is the ground of the possibility of all knowledge,
especially of experience."[26] But we have not, for all that, *become
aware* of that principle; we shall have to limit ourselves to saying
that this synthesis is "represented as *a priori* necessary." For we only
know that "by means of it all objects of possible experience must be
represented *a priori*." Taking things in reverse order and starting
from below (A119), one can show that the *a priori* manifold of space
and time can be reduced to unity only by means of a power of synthesis which does *a priori* what the empirical imagination does in the
association of perceptions. The comparison with the empirical imagination thus provides the transcendental imagination with an ana-
logical sense; but in itself the "third term" remains obscure, hidden,
and blind.

We might well end this reflection on the transcendental imagination, the mediating term in the theoretical order, by saying that the
synthesis it brings about between understanding and sensibility (or
in our terminology, between meaning and appearance, between
speaking and looking) is *consciousness* but that it is not *self-consciousness*. The consciousness philosophy speaks of in its transcendental stage constitutes its own unity only outside of itself, on the
object. When Kant says: "It is clear that . . . the unity which the
object makes necessary can be nothing other than the formal unity
of consciousness in the synthesis of the manifold of representations,"[27] we have to understand conversely that formal unity is
nothing but the condition of possibility of what we called the objectival synthesis. It is in this sense that the transcendental synthesis is
only intentional: it is a unity in intention. We know now what that
means: Consciousness spends itself in founding the unity of meaning and presence "in" the object. "Consciousness" is not yet the unity

26. Ibid., A118, pp. 142–43 [Trans.].
27. Ibid., A105, p. 135 [Trans.].

of a person in itself and for itself; it is not one person; it is no one. The "I" of I think is merely the form of a world for anyone and everyone. It is consciousness in general, that is, a pure and simple project of the object.

It would be a mistake to conclude from this reflection that a philosophy of a transcendental style is empty because it is only formal. It is the first stage of a philosophical anthropology. Whoever would want to commit it to the flames and start right off with a philosophy of the person would leave the *pathétique* only to fall into a fanciful ontology of being and nothingness. If man is a mean between being and nothingness, it is *primarily* because he brings about "mediations" in things; his intermediate place is *primarily* his function as a mediator of the infinite and the finite in things. The transcendental stage is thus the condition of any transposition of the myth of "mélange" and the rhetoric of "misery" into philosophic discourse.

But while the transcendental provides the first moment of a philosophic theory of "disproportion," it remains deficient with respect to the substantial richness of which myth and rhetoric gave a pathetic understanding. There is a surplus that a merely transcendental reflection does not allow us to elevate to the plane of reason.

3

The Practical Synthesis

THE SECOND STAGE of an anthropology of "disproportion" is constituted by the passage from the theoretical to the practical. In what does this passage consist? What calls for it and how does it affect our analysis of "disproportion"?

Roughly speaking, it is a passage from a theory of knowledge to a theory of the will, from the "I think" to the "I will," with its whole cycle of specific determinations: "I desire," "I can," etc.

The sequel to the present analysis will add all the desirable nuances to this massive proposition. For the moment, let us speak of the need to which this new venture of reflection answers.

It answers a concern for totality, a concern that is not given satisfaction by a transcendental reflection. That totality of human reality was, in a certain way, adumbrated in the global vision of the myths of "mélange" and in the rhetoric of "misery." The power of that pathetic understanding was in the very substance that it brought into focus and conveyed. It is this overflow that we are trying to reintegrate into reflection.

When viewed along with the substance adumbrated in the pathetic mode, transcendental reflection seems abstract. Its abstraction is that of the very guide or clue which it has ascribed to itself. Transcendental reflection starts from the *thing*; it is a reflection on the conditions of possibility of the objectivity of the thing. That is its strength and its limitation: its strength because it breaks with the *pathétique* and opens up the properly philosophic dimension of an anthropology; its limitation because the universe of things is still only the abstract framework of our life-world. In order to constitute a world, these things lack all the affective and practical aspects, all the attendant values and counter-values that attract or repel, all the obstacles, the ways and means, tools and instruments that make it practicable or impracticable and, in any event, difficult. This nexus of things especially lacks the presence of persons with whom we work, fight, and communicate, and who stand forth on the horizon of things, on the setting of pragmatic and valorized objects, as other poles of subjectivity, apprehension, valorization, and action. Now, this world of persons expresses itself through the world of things by filling it with new things that are human works.

Accordingly, it is first of all in the *object* that we discern the gap between a transcendental consideration and a totalizing considera- tion. The object, the guide that we have chosen, shows itself to be bare and empty. It is this transcendental guide that requires com- pletion in the strong sense of the word of being made complete.

Do we have to repudiate our starting point? We might be tempted to do so on the pretext that a theory of knowledge that elaborates the "pure" notions of "pure" receptivity, of "pure" concept, of "pure" imagination is posterior to the presence of a complete and concrete person facing a complete and concrete world. But the order of phi- losophy is not a recapitulation of life, existence, or praxis, or how- ever it might be stated. The totality that each of us is and in which we live and act becomes a *problem* only for a philosophy that has made itself aloof from it by asking another question, by giving another foundation to subjectivity, that of the "pure" thing. For such a phi- losophy the totality becomes a *philosophical* problem: that which includes is excluded; that which encompasses is left out. The totality then becomes astonishing; it is the gap, the difference, the remainder. That is why transcendental reflection, though coming late in the move- ment of the totality, must come first in a specifically philosophic order. For this reflection makes the question of the totality philo- sophic by making it problematic.

That is not the only advantage of this procedure. A philosophy that begins in the transcendental mode shows the totality not only as a problem but also as a term of approximation; instead of proceeding straightway toward the totality it approaches it by degrees. Plato had a similar idea when in the *Philebus* he advised against rushing headlong into the abyss of the infinite or into that of the One but recommended learning to linger in between. The true philosopher, he said, is the one "who counts and generates number"; one must not "direct oneself straightway toward the One, but again, to a number that provides thought with a determinate plurality, and come to the One only after having exhausted the whole order."[1]

1. *Philebus* 17e–18a-b.

What Plato said of the One we can apply to the totality. Nothing gives rise to deception more than the idea of totality. All too quickly it has been said: It is here, it is there, it is Mind, it is Nature, it is History. Violence is the next step—first violence to the facts and then violence to man, if, to top it off, the philosopher of totality has power over man.

That explains why our method will consist rather in taking the idea of totality as a task, as a directive idea in the Kantian sense, as a demand for totalization. We shall try to make this demand work in a direction opposed to that of radicality or purity, which regulated our first investigation.

It is from the point of view of an approximation to totality by successive degrees that we must now turn to the theory of the will. In my opinion, such a theory constitutes the principal stage between the "pure" and the "total," the point where the abstract is directed into the concrete. We shall later see why it cannot constitute the last stage.

The greatest advantage that an investigation of totality can draw from the preceding transcendental reflection, which seemed to exclude it, appears now as we introduce this new moment of reflection. Transcendental reflection, as we have seen, is applied to a thematic structure that is more fundamental than reflection, namely, that of disproportion and intermediacy. Reflection has endowed this thematic structure with philosophic status by capturing it in the notions of perspective, meaning, and synthesis. This triad will be the melodic germ of all the subsequent developments. Taken as a totality, human reality will appear to us as a progressively richer and more complete dialectic between more and more concrete poles and in mediations that become progressively closer to life. But we shall try to understand all the other forms of human polarity and mediation in function of the notions of *perspective* and *meaning*, notions elaborated on the transcendental level. Thus the approach to the human totality will not be given over to hazard and fancy. It will be illuminated and oriented by the transcendental theme of synthesis.

From this transcendentally guided approach we expect to obtain the full notion of fallibility. Accordingly, we shall maintain the following:

All the aspects of "practical" finitude that can be understood on the basis of the transcendental notion of perspective may be summed up in the notion of character. All the aspects of "practical" infinitude that can be understood on the basis of the transcendental notion of meaning may be summed up in the notion of happiness. The "practical" mediation that extends the mediation of the transcendental imagination, projected into the object, is the constitution of the person by means of "respect." This new analysis aims at showing the fragility of this practical mediation of respect, for which the person is the correlate.

In this new stage the "person" and no longer the "thing" is the object that serves us as a guide. This object provokes the same kind of reflective regression as what led from the constitution of the thing to the synthesis of the transcendental imagination. Here it is *respect* that will show its inner duality. But behind this ethical duality, we must discover the roots of practical disproportion. In order to go back to the primordial practical moment, prior to an ethics of the "fallen," we shall try to uncover, on a level that is more radical than any moral dualism, the "disproportion" of character and happiness.

CHARACTER

All the aspects of "practical" finitude that can be understood on the basis of the transcendental notion of finite perspective may be summed up in the notion of character.

But the notion of character must itself be approached by degrees. Indeed, character is, in a way, a totalization of all the aspects of finitude. To avoid turning character into a "thing" or a "fate," we must carefully compose the notion of it, beginning with that of perspective.

(a) Affective Perspective

What makes the notion of perspective so abstract is primarily the absence of affective features in the wholly "pure" idea of point of view. One might say that point of view is a "disinterested" perspective, a simple angle of vision or narrowness of scope that expresses the limitation of a "here." Point of view is an affectively *neutralized* perspective. Accordingly, we must first of all restore the affective aspect of perspective.

Let us try to reconstitute the reflective procedure by which I may bring this new aspect of narrowness or closing to the focus of attention. In point of fact, I am not turned toward my affective perspective; on the contrary, it is out of it that things appear interesting to me; and it is upon these things that I grasp the lovable, the attractive, the hateful, the repulsive. Moreover, these affective aspects of the thing are themselvs involved as motivating agents in the practical dispositions of my will. It is by means of a will which is nourished with *motives* and which *projects* and is projected that my affective life unfolds its spontaneous or reflective evaluations. The lovable and the hateful are stages in this anticipatory activity that we call the project. And so, far from noticing the narrowness of my affective perspective, I am at first given over entirely to what I am doing; and what I do is interpolated into my project of what is to be done. Thus in pre-reflective naïveté, I am turned first toward the projected work, toward the *pragma*.

Therefore, we must disengage motivation from the project[2] and disengage affective finitude from motivation.

2. I am referring to the analyses set forth in *Le Volontaire et l'Involontaire*. There I stressed the affective rootedness of the will, following Aristotle's excellent formula: "The will moves through desire." The force of this analysis was then directed against philosophies that overvalue the moment of the welling up or surging forth of choice. If it is true that I determine *myself*, that I decide *myself*, and that this relation which is both active and reflexive of self to self already contains an implicit judgment of attribution, we must say as a counterpart that this self-attribution does not constitute the fundamental operation of the will. What makes the Self spring to the center of reflection is a second-order movement, an act of recovery, of return, of self-recognition. The will's first action, however, is not this movement of reiteration by which I attribute my acts to myself, but the one by which I posit them. Now, the movement of the self, in its pre-reflective naïveté, lies in the intentional moment through which I array before me the "to-be-done-by-me" through which I break through to the world of possibilities, of eventualities, of novel events. I am not, therefore, at first directed toward my power to be but toward the object of my projects that I defined as follows: "Decision signifies, that is, designates emptily, a future action which depends on me and which lies within my power" (p. 42).

Following this definition of project, I proposed a definition of motivation that is more precise than that found in contemporary psychology where motivation covers the notion of motivation in the strict sense of a motive *of*

Motivation brings into view a new kind of "receptivity" wherein my finitude is inscribed. It is no longer the sensory receptivity of seeing and hearing, but the specific receptivity which signifies that I do not create my projects radically from nothing, no more than I produce my objects through creative intuition. I posit actions only by letting myself be influenced by motives. I advance toward . . . (toward the "to be done") only by supporting myself *upon* . . . (upon the lovable, the hateful, etc.). A human freedom is one that advances by means of motivated projects. I *constitute* my actions to the extent that I *gather in* reasons for them.

For the first time we see in what sense the analysis of perspective is a transcendental guide for all the other aspects of finitude: because sensory receptivity is the first form of receptivity admitting of transcendental reflection, it serves as an analogue for all the others. First of all, it serves as an analogue for motivation: "I see" why I act in such a way; "I hear" the call of the desirable and the lovable.

But the metaphors borrowed from the sphere of "receptivity" constituted by perceiving must not conceal the new features of the receptivity of desire: it is a "practical" receptivity and no longer a "theoretical" one; a receptivity commensurable with a project, no longer with a vision. That is why the name that best describes it is "inclination" in the strong and classical sense of the word which gives us the expression "to incline without necessitating." Inclination is the specific "passion" of the will. Only an inclined, aroused will can also determine *itself*. Its activity is imbued with this specific passivity.

Accordingly, if *desire* is a form of receptivity, analogous to that of perception but different and new, in what does its finitude consist?

Shall we say that the human will is *finite* by the very fact that it is not pure act but a motivated project, action–passion? We may remember that a similar question was asked with regard to perception: Are we finite because we have to receive our objects in order to form them? We had to reply that sensory receptivity reveals first its openness and that finitude is the narrowness of this openness, namely, the *perspectival* aspect of our way of being affected.

---

willing, therefore in its relation to a project, to a work "to be done," what ordinary language expresses in the relation of "because": I intend to . . . because. . . . Taken in this precise sense, motivation is a structure of voluntary decision.

The analysis of desire proposes the same relation between opening and closing, between vision of the world and point of view.

Desire does not show me *my* way of being affected, nor does it shut me up within my desiring self. It does not speak to me at first of myself because it is not at first a way of being aware of *myself*, even less an "internal sensation." It is an experienced lack of . . . , an impulse oriented toward. . . .[3] In desire I am outside myself; I am with the desirable in the world. In short, in desire I am open to all the affective tones of things that attract or repel me. It is this attraction, grasped on the thing itself, over there, elsewhere, or nowhere, which makes desire an openness onto . . . and not a presence to the self closed on itself.

If we now move back from the worldly tones of the desirable toward the desiring body, we must say once again that the body, the flesh of desire, does not manifest itself as a closed figure but as a practical mediation, in other words as a *projecting body* in the same sense that we were able to speak of the *perceiving body*. My flesh of desire is wholly anticipation, that is, a prefigured grasp or hold, over there, elsewhere, nowhere, outside myself. The desiring body steals away in advance, proffering the *élan* of its flesh to the projecting self.

Where is finitude in all of this? A difficult change-over to the obscure must now extricate from the aim of desire something like the affective equivalent of what was perspective for the perceiving body. Perspective, we remember, was intertwined with the intentional aim of perception; it was the zero origin of all the successive views grasped first on one side and then on the other side of the thing. Desire proposes a similar regression starting from its intentional aspects. Finitude is here the confusion or the opacity that darkens what we might call the clarity of desire.

It may seem strange to speak of the clarity of desire, but its intentionality is just that. Desire is a lack *of* . . . , a drive *toward*. . . . The "of" and the "toward" indicate the oriented and elective character of desire. This specific aspect of desire, taken as desire of "this" or of "that," is susceptible of being elucidated—in the precise sense of the word—by the light of its representation. Human desire illuminates its aim through the representation of the absent thing, of how

3. I am not making a decision here between the Cartesian interpretation as negative (lack, privation) and the Spinozist interpretation as positive (*conatus*, self-affirmation). See *Le Volontaire et l'Involontaire*, pp. 88–89.

it may be reached, and the obstacles which block its attainment. These imaging forms direct desire upon the world; I take pleasure in them; in them I am out of myself. The image is even more; not only does it anticipate the perceptual outlines of gestual behavior, but it also anticipates pleasure and pain, the joy and sadness of being joined to or separated from the desired object. This imaging affectivity, held in pledge by the affective effigy or by the representative or analogue of future pleasure, ends by bringing me in imagination to the goal of desire. Here the image is nothing other than desire. The image informs desire, lays it open, and illuminates it. Through the image, desire enters into the field of motivation. From the standpoint of value, desire may be compared to other motives and thereby sacrificed or privileged, approved or reproved.

In this sense we can speak of a light of affectivity or a clarity of desire. It is nothing other than its affective aim. My body, traversed, so to speak, by this intention, outruns itself. It becomes a mediator of projects or, as Descartes says, it "disposes [the soul] to wish for the future the things which it represents to itself as agreeable."[4]

However, if desire is clear insofar as it imagines, it is at the same time *confused*: it is this confusion inhering in the clarity of desire which avers the finitude of it. There is an impregnable opacity that does not "pass" into the image, not only into the image of the thing or into the image of ways, means, and obstacles, but even into the imagined anticipation of the joy of being "joined by the will" to the desired thing.

What, then, is this affective opacity, and what does it signify for man's being, insofar as this being is openness? One might well say that it is the reverse or the underside of the intentionality of desire, therefore that in the aim which does not aim and that in choice which does not choose. It is a way one "feels" or "the mood in which one finds oneself,"[5] which actually desires nothing, nothing else and nothing definite, a total and undivided experience of my body that is no longer traversed by all its intentions toward the world but turned back into itself, no longer a mediator but feeling itself. Coenesthesis is precisely this.

4. *The Passions of the Soul*, art. 86.
5. *Se sentir* and *se trouver bien ou mal*. The latter renders Heidegger's *Befindlichkeit*, the "way" or "mood" in which we "find" ourselves. Cf. *Sein und Zeit*, §§ 29–30 [Trans.].

If we compare this analysis with the previous one, it turns out that what we called point of view, zero origin, and center of perspective, with respect to the perceiving body, is what we now call coenesthesis or confusion.

The way one "feels," or "finding oneself in a certain mood," bestows upon the perceiving body, on point of view, a density that is the false profundity of existence, the body's dumb and inexpressible presence to itself. The "here" of my body, manifested in the opaque feeling, vibrates its presence. That "deep" sensibility shows that my body is still something besides the letting-in of the world or the letting-be of all things. The body is not pure mediation; it is still immediate for itself and in this way seals up its intentional openness.

The fact that the body cannot be a pure mediator but is also immediately for itself constitutes its affective closing.

Along with this affective closing we discover the feeling of the primal difference between the I and all others; to find oneself in a certain mood is to feel one's individuality as inexpressible and incommunicable. Just as one's position cannot be shared with another, so also the affective situation in which I find myself and feel myself cannot be exchanged. It is here that egoism, as well as vice, finds its opportunity: out of difference or otherness it makes a preference. But self-preference finds that inherent in every inclination is what the Stoics called a self-attachment, an innate tendency to will oneself good, a love of one's own make-up, what I would readily call self-love as point of view.[6]

As the Stoics saw it, every desire "of *something*" involves a "feeling and dilection of oneself." This adhesion to oneself is the continuo, the unitive bond of all affective aims, multiple and diversified through their objects. What we called the subject-pole of all perceptions now thickens into self-love. The center for which all things are and from which all things appear is no longer merely the zero origin of looking but is rather self-attachment. Dire circumstances bring welling up to the center of a situation that dilection of myself which is only dully present to the desire of something: let my life as a whole be threatened, let me be in danger of death, and all that is desirable spread throughout the world comes back upon this first desirable

6. *De Finibus* 3.5: "Fieri autem non posset, ut appeterent aliquid, nisi sensum haberent sui eoque se et sua diligerent."

which turns from implicit self-love to the will to live. And my fear of dying and my desire to survive cry out to me: "Stay, dear, unique, irreplaceable point of view!"

Such is *affective* finitude, difference in love with itself.

(b) Practical Perspective

This same mark of "closing" is found a second time in the *powers* that serve the will. Not, once again, that inflexibility, intractability, or the inaptitude for change which wont confers on habitual behaviors are the primary characteristics of my powers. On the contrary, openness is the first and direct signification of the human being among the beings of the world, and finitude is always the reverse. In the course of performing an action my body is traversed; it is not the terminus of action, the πράγμα, but the ὄργανον. This relation of organ to action, which is, moreover, irreducible to the relation of a mechanical instrument to an exterior agent, is the relation we catch sight of in human actions executed with ease and grace. In order for attention to turn back upon the actuated organ and to detach itself from the work being done, which, in a certain way, draws the body along the action-pattern, a particular circumstance must be encountered: that of meeting a resistance. Then the actuated body, the primal mediator between the acting self and the acted-upon world, becomes the focus of the situation and exhibits its *practical* finitude.

Every power has a reverse side of impotence. On the one hand, the acquisition of habits liberates attention by entrusting action to habitual systems that start and unwind like supervised automatisms. Thus the body is a node of powers, of motor and affective structures, of interchangeable methods whose spontaneity is at the disposal of the will. It is enough to watch our familiar gestures in action to see how the body leads the way, tries out and invents, answers our expectations or eludes us.

This practical mediation of the body extends beyond *motor* habits in the strict sense. Our skills are also a kind of body, a psychical body, as it were: through rules of grammar and arithmetic, through social sophistication and moral knowledge we learn and form new skills. In all ways of learning, bodily and intellectual, there is this relation of an action to an enacted body, of a will to a power set in motion.

Now, it is the same practical spontaneity, mediator of all our volitions, which makes of my power my impotence. Indeed, every habit is the start of an alienation that is inscribed in the very structure of habit, in the relation between *learning* and *contracting*. Habit is possible because the living person has the admirable power of changing himself through his acts. But by learning, man affects himself; his subsequent power is in the situation no longer of beginning but of continuing; life goes on, and beginning is rare. Thus there arises, through this continued affecting of myself, a kind of human nature—that is, an imitation of the native, of the innate, by the habitual. What is learned is acquired (*habitudo*), and what is acquired is contracted. Habit, then, takes on in the course of living the opposite signification of emotion, which, according to Descartes' admirable intuition in the *Passions of the Soul*, commences and recommences in "surprise." Habit *fixes* our tastes and aptitudes and thus shrinks our field of availability; the range of the possible narrows down; my life has taken shape. This is not to say that true habits are automatisms; on the contrary, the most flexible and interchangeable habits, those closest to systematic arrangement or method, best illustrate what Ravaisson called the return of freedom to nature. For it is precisely at the expense of the availability of these plastic habits, which do not have the rigidity of mechanical systems, that the counter-process of "sclerosis" develops. That is why our habits are very ambiguous; it is not by chance that they lend themselves to two opposing systems of interpretation, in terms of life that "learns" and life that "automatizes," in terms of spontaneity and inertia.

This tendency of life to harden into set systems and imitate the thing bids us to look for the new mode of finitude in a primordial inertia that is intermingled with the spontaneity of life and will; it is as though, because of our body, we were subjected to a law of materiality present on all levels of reality. In naturalizing itself, said Ravaisson, freedom bears out "the primordial law and the most general form of being, the tendency to persevere in the very act that constitutes being."[7] Practical finitude is this form of perseverance.

7. Ravaisson, *De l'habitude*, p. 22.

This new aspect of finitude is no greater a woe than the preceding aspects: this inertia is the converse of my power. No will without power, no power that is not a contracted form. No present Cogito without a past and abolished Cogito, which has become a knowing and a having, and in that sense not current. Ravaisson understood better than anyone this dialectic of *available power* and *contracted form* in the heart of Habit.[8]

One could return to the same themes starting from an analysis of time and show the same dialectic of innovation and sedimentation.

We see, then, that finitude is, first, perspective, then self-dilection, and then inertia or form of perseverance. Or in other words, if we wished to generalize the idea of perspective beyond its nucleus of sense—that is, beyond its use in the phenomenology of perception— we could say that self-love and the customary form that my existence "contracts" constitute the affective and practical perspective of my existence.

(c) Character

These various aspects of finitude—perspective, primal self-dilection, perseverance, and inertia—come together in the notion of character. What the latter adds to them is the idea of a totality, the finite totality of my existence. Character is the finite openness of my existence taken as a whole.

But how can I look upon my existence as a finite totality? Is this limitation different from a quantitative one? It does not seem so, at least not to common sense that sees in character nothing other than the possibility each person provides for others of sketching his "portrait." Now, the portrait is at once a *closed* figure, a closed circuit that detaches the form from the substance and a finite sum of distinctive marks drawn up by an alien spectator. This metaphor of the "portrait" orients us toward a wholly inexact idea of character and its type of finitude. When it is badly understood, characterology itself is liable to support the illusion that one could reconstruct character with a finite number of simple components such as emotivity, activity, secondariness combined in various ways. But this characterological formula of finitude expresses only the impotence of

8. See *Le Volontaire et l'Involontaire*, p. 310..

our abstract combinatory; it points up the poverty of stereotypes, of those "creatures of the mind" which aid the pragmatic recognition of an individual and allow us to expect a certain behavior from him. In comparison to the finitude of the characterological formula the individual is infinite; such a formula, indeed, remains dependent on classificatory thinking. For, as Kant understood it, the law of specification requires the endless division of genera into species and subspecies because no species can be regarded as being in itself the lowest species.[9]

If, therefore, the finitude of character is not that of the characterological formula in a science of characters, then what is it?

Here we must try to interpret the idea of character through that of perspective or point of view which originally seemed linked to the idea of openness. This alone can make us understand that character is a limitation inherent in the mediating function of one's own body, the primal narrowness of my openness.

But how can we pass from the idea of perspective to that of character? My perspective was a *perceptual* finitude, that is, the finite aspect of my openness onto the world taken as a world of *things*. Thus the concept of point of view was correlative to the appearance of certain *constants of appearance* that Hegel calls the "tranquil result" into which becoming sinks. The flux of appearance threads itself onto the concretions of becoming, to centers of reality, and my life of consciousness overspills itself and settles in these real unities. My primary belief goes to them.

Thus the notion of perspective designated my finitude relative to the thingness of the "thing." Perspective is my finitude for the thing.

How can we speak of finitude in all respects? We must trace back a path from the exterior portrait, from the characterological formula to the stylistic unity, the physiognomical value of character "in the first person." That is not utterly impossible if we are attentive to the revealing purport of "expressions" in the broad sense of the word. Bergson, in his famous analysis of the free act, caught a glimpse of all that philosophic reflection could reap from these acts and feelings, "each of which represents the entire soul, in the sense that the whole content of the soul is reflected in each of them." Between certain expressive acts and "the whole personality" there is, he says,

9. *Critique of Pure Reason,* "The Regulative Employment of the Ideas of Pure Reason," A656.

"that undefinable resemblance that one sometimes finds between the artist and his work." The question of whether or not these highly expressive acts are precisely what one looks for under the name of free act does not interest us here. What does interest us is only the totality that is revealed through them. The astonishing thing is that character is a totality that is given only in the adumbrations of an expression. Certain feelings are expressive in this sense: "Each of us has his way of loving and hating, and this love and hate reflect his whole personality." The "depth" of the feeling is nothing else than this power of total expression: "Each of these feelings, provided they have attained a sufficient depth, represents the whole soul." Character—Bergson says, the personality—is to be found in its entirety in a single one of them, "provided one knows how to choose it."

This totality, manifested through a single act or one well-chosen feeling, could be called *the total field of motivation* (which Bergson again suggests by his excellent phrase: "our personal idea of happiness or honor"). The idea of field of motivation has a less ethical and more psychological turn than the Bergsonian idea. Moreover, it has the advantage of reminding us that character is by no means a portrait that one can draw from the outside, but that it must be caught in one of those highly expressive acts, one of those deep feelings which I experience in myself or understand in others.

What, then, is the finitude of character? Far from being a bounded thing it is the *limited openness of our field of motivation taken as a whole*. In this way we apply the dialectic of openness and closure, formulated in connection with the perspective of perception, to the notion of a total field of motivation attained by means of expression. After the detour through the idea of perspective, character, which elsewhere we called the finite manner of freedom, now appears to us as the perspectival orientation of our field of motivation taken as a whole.

This connection between openness and closure on the level of the "whole soul" can be made explicit in the following way: the openness of my field of motivation is my fundamental accessibility to all values of all men in all cultures. My field of motivation is open to the whole range of the human. This is the meaning of the famous statement: "Nothing human is foreign to me." I am capable of every virtue and every vice; no sign of man is radically incomprehensible, no language radically untranslatable, no work of art to which my taste cannot spread. My humanity is my essential community with all that is human outside myself; that community makes every man my like.

My character is not the opposite of that humanity; my character is that humanity seen from somewhere, the whole city seen from a certain angle, the partial totality. Alain understood better than anyone the paradoxal synthesis of the universal and the singular in the person: "In every human body all passions and errors are possible.... Yet this is true in accordance with an inimitable formula of life that each man has unto himself. There are as many ways of being wicked and unhappy as there are men in the world. But there is also a salvation peculiar to each man, of the same complexion, of the same turn as he." All values are accessible to all men, but in a way that is peculiar to each one. It is in this sense that "each" man is "man."

That is why my character is never perceived in itself, no more than the origin of perception is itself the object of perception. I do not aim at "my" personal idea of happiness and honor but happiness and honor *per se*; "my" character is implied in the humanity of my individual existence as the zero origin of my field of motivation; nor do I meet it as an exterior boundary, for it is not a fate that governs my life from the outside but the inimitable way in which I exercise my freedom as a man. I read my character and designate it only through allusion, in the feeling of otherness that makes me different from all others; or rather, different from those like me, for another is a like man but a different character. Consequently, I can no more seize the individuality of a character apart from its universal humanity than I can separate the narrowness of a perceptual point of view from its openness onto a panorama of objects and, beyond these, onto an horizon of endless perceptibility.

Character is the narrowness of the "whole soul" whose humanity is openness. My character and my humanity together make of my freedom an unlimited possibility and a constituted partiality.

The idea of a constituted partiality will help us to take a final step. Character, we said, is not a fate that governs me from the outside. And yet in a certain way it is a fate, and in a twofold way: first as unalterable, then as received and inherited.

How can we introduce these two "destinal" aspects of character without reducing it again to a thing? One last reflection on the theme of perspective will help us here.

The immutability of character is ultimately nothing other than the most radical and primordial aspect of the idea of perspectival origin. The zero origin of perception, what we call our point of view, is not yet a true origin. I can change the origin of all my views; it is a matter of movement. But if I can change my position, I cannot change my character. *There is no movement by which I could change the zero origin of my total field of motivation.* There is not even a spiritual movement that has the power to alter the origin of my most fundamental evaluations. The most radical conversion could not amount to a change of character without making me not only a "new creature" but a *different* individual: my life may be oriented by a new constellation of fixed stars, that is, by a new nucleus of values that are not brought into question by the mediate and more intimate values of everyday living. But it is still with the same hand and the same turn, as Alain said, that I will be generous and that I will have been miserly.

In this way I attain the idea of an *immobile* source, in the literal sense, of all my *changes* of point of view, of an immutable perspective, in the sense that I cannot "enter" it nor could I "leave" it. It is in this sense that my character is the radically non-chosen origin of all my choices.

In making the transition from character as immutable to character as inherited we may go through the following consideration.

If I cannot change my character, if I can neither choose nor repudiate its perspective, then character is not only immutable but indistinguishable from the *fact* of my existence. What do I mean by calling my character a fact? I mean that as far back as I remember, I was *already* this finite openness onto the universal human condition. To this situation, there is no beginning that belongs to consciousness and is capable of being retrieved in a choosing of myself. All points of view originate from this non-posited source of all my assumed positions; my character is not the result of taking a position.

Now this is exactly what is meant when I say that I was *born*. My birth designates the primary fact that my existence is itself a fact. For others it was an event; for me it is the limit fleeing beyond the reach of my earliest recollections, the ever-earlier beginning toward which the faltering memory of my infancy is driven. This event for others draws my attention to my state of being already born. My birth therefore is nothing other than my character; to say that I was born is merely to point to my character as that which I find. My birth betokens the "having been," the mark of the past that clings to the state of existing. My birth is the already–there-ness of my character.

For this primordial origin to appear to me as an exterior fate, as an irrevocable decree that weighs on my life from the outside, I have only to oppose it to myself, treat it as an object, and, consequently, forget its function as an origin of perspective. In this way there arises that caricature of character which we called the portrait or the characterological formula. But we had to go the long roundabout way via the perspectival interpretation of character to discover fate itself as a function of existence in the first person.

My birth, however, speaks to me in another way of my existence as received: not only found *here* but given through *others*. I was brought into the world; I am descended from my parents; they form my lineage. I do not know the meaning of this gift that makes me heir to my own life. Here more than anywhere the vertigo of objectification threatens me. When I think of my ancestors as outside of me, my birth suddenly seems like one combination among others. My existence, thus replaced in the field of objective encounters, at first seems fortuitous, arbitrary, trivial, even improbable; then, in the next moment, granting all the encounters, it seems to me that I am no more than the necessary result of all these intersectings, the bearer of a hereditary capital that totally alienates my freedom. This mélange of *contingency* in encounters and of *necessity* in the result is precisely the fate of birth.

This "heredity," however, which tells me that I am dependent at the very origin of all my projects of autonomy, must not be placed outside of me or in front of me, as was the case with character a little while ago. My heredity is my character insofar as it is received from another. My character is the primal orientation of my total field of motivation, and this field is my openness to humanity. Thus, step by step the most "destinal" aspects of finitude are recaptured in the dialectic of narrowness and accessibility to which the perspective of perception has given us the key.

Philosophic understanding does not progress by going from the objectively known heredity to the perspective that is subjectively apprehended as behind the perceived sight. It goes from this proffered and open sight to its perspectival origin, and the latter becomes progressively enriched with all the practical, affective aspects that culminate in the notion of character, of immutable and inherited nature.

Then the fate of character and heredity discloses its meaning: it is the given, factual narrowness of my free openness to the full range of the possibilities of the being man.

The "disproportion" between sense and perspective, between intending and looking, between the verb and the point of view, is as the melodic germ of all the variations and all the developments that culminate in the "disproportion" between happiness and character.

This "disproportion," we remember, vouched for itself in the simple fact of reflection. Man's finitude, we said, is such that it can be known and expressed; and it can be expressed only because speaking itself is already a transgression of point of view and finite perspective. However, that "disproportion" between speaking and perspective was still only the theoretical aspect of human disproportion. What we are trying to express now is the *global* character of disproportion.

In this attempt at totalization we can take as a guide the intermediary procedures that led us to totalize the various facets of finitude in the finitude of character.

Indeed, what we are aiming at with the term happiness is not a particular form of transgression or human transcendence but the total aim of all the facets of transgression: "Every art and every inquiry, and similarly every action and pursuit," says Aristotle, "seems to aim at some good. Consequently the Good has rightly been said to be that at which all things aim."[10] But in that case, we must question the function of man (τὸ ἔργον τοῦ ἀνθρώπου)[11] in its undividedness and totality.

Now, I cannot grasp that "function of man" straightway. I must gradually develop it out of the theoretical concept of Meaning; otherwise what I designate by the term happiness would never be the supreme good, that is, "that for whose sake everything else is done." Happiness would be only the vague dream of the "agreeableness of life, which, without interruption, accompanies the whole of existence" (the expression comes from Kant, and it is not by chance that we evoke it at this point). In short, happiness would be not a totality

10. *Nicomachean Ethics* I, 1, 1094a 1–4.
11. Ibid. 1097b 25.

of meaning and contentment, but merely a sum of pleasure, or, as Kant says, a material principle of the faculty of desiring.

Accordingly, there is a first, naïve idea of happiness that must be *reduced* in order to disclose its full meaning. This naïve idea is the one that flows from an immediate analysis of human acts taken individually: these acts aim toward a consciousness of result—satisfaction or suppression of pain—wherein action finds a temporary repose. The rambling imagination prolongs this moment of repose *indefinitely*; thinking to eternalize it, imagination stretches it out and perpetuates it; it remains in the indefinitely finite perspective of self-dilection. Happiness is something entirely different; it is not a finite term but must be to the aggregate of human aims what the world is to the aims of perception. Just as the world is the horizon of *the thing*, happiness is the horizon from every point of view. The world is not the horizon from every point of view but only the counterpart of one kind of finitude and one kind of attitude: my finitude and my attitude with regard to the thing. The idea of the world is total only in one dimension; it is an infinite in only one genus, the genus of the thing; but the "thing" is an abstraction from integral reality. For this reason we must go beyond the idea of world toward the most far-reaching idea conceivable, one that is fuller than we experience it to be, as Descartes said of the will.

It is here that an immediate analysis of human desire that would try to do without the transcendental stage of reflection falls short. Such an analysis lacks the means to distinguish the totality of completion that the "function of man" aims at from the feeling that is prolonged in the imagination of having attained a result, fulfilled a program, or overcome a difficulty. This can be seen quite clearly in the Aristotelian analysis of happiness: the Stagirite restricts himself to discriminating happiness in the *de facto* aim of human desire: "The principle in this matter," he says, "is the fact." Direct psychological reflection, however, cannot distinguish the totality of completion from a mere sum of pleasures: the "highest good," the "unique desirable," remains intermixed with "good living."

That is why Kant had to begin by excluding happiness from the search for the "principle" of morality by relegating it to the power of desiring and identifying it with self-love: "a rational being's consciousness of the agreeableness of life which without interruption accompanies his whole existence is happiness, and to make this the

supreme ground for the determination of choice constitutes the principle of self-love."[12] And again, "To be happy is necessarily the
desire of every rational but finite being."[13]

But this ἐποχή of happiness, understood as the lasting agreeableness of life, restores the authentic problem of happiness, now considered as a totality of completion.

Indeed, it is not the "faculty of desiring" that we must question,
but what Aristotle called the human ἔργον, that is, man's existential
project considered as an indivisible whole. The investigation of human action and its all-embracing and most ultimate aim would disclose that happiness is a termination of destiny and not an end of
individual desires. It is in this sense that it is a *whole* and not a *sum*;
the partial aims and disconnected desires of our life stand out on
its horizon.

But how shall I pass from the idea of a sum to that of a whole?
Man's function, insofar as it is distinct from the sum of his partial
intentions, would elude me if I could not connect the movement of
the whole to the very project of reason, which is that in me which
demands the totality. This demand for totality or reason[14] is what
allows me to distinguish happiness as the supreme good from happiness as an accumulation of fulfilled desires. For the totality "demanded" by "reason" is also the one that the human act "pursues."
The Kantian *Verlangen* (demand, exigency, request) is the transcendental revealer of the meaning of the Aristotelian ἐφίεσθαι (pursuit, tendency, quest). That "demand," Kaut says, loses itself in
illusion. But the origin of this very illusion is "a view [*Aussicht*] into
a higher immutable order of things in which we already are, and in
which we may, by definite precepts, continue our existence in accordance with the supreme decree of reason."[15] This dense and admirable text—this "view into," this "order in which we already are,"
this continuation of our existence in accordance with the destination
or assignation of reason—is it not that totality of *contentment* which
we are looking for under the name of happiness, but filtered, so to
speak, by the demand for a totality of *meaning* that is reason? It is

12. *Critique of Practical Reason*, trans. L. W. Beck (Chicago: University
of Chicago Press, 1949), p. 133 [Trans.].
    13. Ibid., p. 136.
    14. Ibid., p. 212.
    15. Ibid., p. 212 (translation changed).

true that Kant does not yet call it happiness, but the "entire object of a pure practical reason."[16] It is this "entire object" of practical reason which demands that the idea of happiness be redeemed; excluded from the principle of morality, it is now connected to the dialectic of pure, practical reason, that is, to the completion of morality and the eschatology of freedom. No doubt in Kantianism the idea of happiness is conserved only as merited happiness and not as desired happiness. Without underestimating the importance of this moralization of happiness, can we not put the emphasis on the demand of reason that shows virtue alone to be unequal to that "entire object" of reason, rather than on the moral coloring of happiness by the virtue that *merits* it? Whether virtue *merits* happiness is less important than the fact that reason demands the joining of happiness to virtue for the good to be complete and perfect: "For to be in need of happiness and also worthy of it and yet not to partake of it could not be in accordance with the complete volition of an omnipotent rational being, if we assume such only for the sake of the argument."[17]

I who am finite perspective, dilection of my body, habit and inertia, character, am capable of conceiving a "complete volition of an omnipotent rational being." Or to go back to a Kantian expression that we used above, I am the bearer of the "supreme destination of reason" in accordance with which I can "continue my existence." The idea of a complete volition and the destination of reason hollow an infinite depth in my desire, making it the desire for happiness and not merely the desire for pleasure.

The idea of totality, therefore, is not merely a rule for theoretical thought. It dwells in the human will and in this way becomes the source of the most extreme "disproportion": that which preys on human *action* and strains it between the finitude of character and the infinitude of happiness.

How does this "disproportion" appear?

As we have seen, character is never looked upon; it is not an object but an origin. It is following the finite manner of my character that I open myself to the human in its entirety. Everything human—ideas, beliefs, values, signs, works, tools, institutions—is within my reach in accordance with the finite perspective of an absolutely individual form of life. When I come before the signs of man I do not think of

16. Ibid., p. 214.
17. Ibid., p. 215.

my character or my individuality, but the humanity of those signs. My character is the zero origin of my thinking; I attain it only by means of a kind of reflective allusion to the narrowness of my field of attention.

My experience evinces happiness in another way, diametrically opposed to the preceding one. Just as I receive indications of my perceptual narrowness—if only through being at variance with others—I also receive signs of my destination to happiness. These are privileged experiences, precious moments in which I receive the assurance that I am on the right path. Suddenly the horizon is clear, unlimited possibilities open up before me; the feeling of the "immense" then replies dialectically to the feeling of the "narrow."

Let us come back to the notion of total field of motivation, which was useful in suggesting the idea of character. It refers to nothing other than an instantaneous cross-section of what we earlier called "man's function" or his "existential project." We may say, then, that the total field of motivation is an *oriented* field. Character is the zero origin of this field orientation; happiness is its infinite end. This image makes us understand that happiness is not given in any experience; it is only adumbrated in a consciousness of direction. No act gives happiness, but the encounters of our life that are most worthy of being called "events" indicate the direction of happiness. Thévenaz reminds us that "a meaningful direction is inherent in any event: an event is an event only because it *is* a meaningful direction and is recognized as such."[18] The events that bespeak happiness are those which remove obstacles and uncover a vast landscape of existence. The excess of meaning, the overflow, the immense: that is the sign that we are "directed toward" happiness.

However, I could not make out these signs or interpret them as "transcending anticipations" of happiness[19] if reason, in me, were not the demand for totality. Reason demands totality, but the instinct for happiness, insofar as it is a feeling that anticipates its realization more than it provides it, assures me that I am *directed toward* the very thing that reason *demands*. Reason opens up the dimension

18. P. Thévenaz, *L'Homme et sa raison* (Neuchâtel, 1956), II 136 [*il n'y a d'événements que sensé: c'est parce qu'il est un sens, est un sens reconnu, qu'il est événement*. The French *sens* can be taken as direction, meaning, sense. Trans.].

19. S. Strasser, *Das Gemüt* (Utrecht & Freiburg, 1956), pp. 238ff.

of totality, but the consciousness of direction, experienced in the feeling of happiness, assures me that this reason is not alien to me, that it coincides with my destiny, that it is interior to it and, as it were, coeval with it.

RESPECT

Can there be a synthesis of happiness and character? Most assuredly, and that synthesis is found in the person. The person is the *Self* that was lacking to the "I" of the Kantian "I think," to consciousness in general, the correlate of the synthesis of the object.

One would be greatly mistaken, however, in holding this synthesis for an accomplished one, given in itself in the immediacy of self to self. The person is still a projected synthesis that seizes itself in the representation of a task, of an ideal of what the person should be. The Self is aimed at rather than experienced. Indeed, the person is not yet consciousness of Self for Self; it is consciousness of self only in the representation of the ideal of the Self. There is no experience of the person in itself and for itself.

Accordingly we must proceed with the practical synthesis as we did with the theoretical synthesis. First, we must take as a guide this new, represented, and projected object that constitutes the person's personality, in the same way as we grounded ourselves on the constitution of the thing, such as we objectify it for ourselves. Only then will it be possible to proceed reflectively and to look for the conditions of the person's personality.

Man's fragility will appear to us for the second time in this reflective movement. This fragility comes out in the nascent dissociation of the new "intermediary" in which the practical synthesis is realized. An analysis similar to that of the transcendental imagination, an "art concealed in the depths of nature," recommends itself to us, and at the end of this analysis the phenomenology of fallibility will have accomplished its second decisive step. But at the same time it will be seen that this second step cannot be the last one, since our reflection will have remained quite formal, having escaped a transcendental formalism only to enter upon a practical formalism, that of the idea of the person.

What we must first establish is that the person is primarily a project which I represent to myself, which I set before me and entertain, and that this project of the person is, like the thing but in an entirely irreducible way, a "synthesis" which is effected.

This project is what I call *humanity*, not in the collective sense of all men but the human quality of man, not an exhaustive enumeration of human beings but the comprehensive significance of the human element that is capable of guiding and regulating an enumeration of human beings.

Humanity is the person's personality, just as objectivity was the thing's thingness; it is the mode of being on which every empirical appearance of what we call a human being should be patterned. In Heideggerian language it is the ontological constitution of human "beings."[20]

It is this constitution that I am projecting when I think man and when I proclaim the human.

In what does this constitution of the being man consist? Strictly speaking, we know already, since we were able to formulate the two antithetical notions of character and happiness only in function of man's project and in drawing upon that project. In the same fashion, we were able to elaborate the notions of meaning and perspective only by starting from the thing and on the thing, considering alternately how it affects me by its unilateral appearances, its silhouettes, and how I think it in the unity of its supposed, signified, and expressed meaning.

Likewise, it is *on* the idea of man that we discovered what we called affective perspective, practical perspective, and finally the individual perspective of character that is nothing but the narrowness of my access to all values of all men in all cultures. Thus we have been able to reflect character only in function of an idea, a badly thematized one, that of a field of motivation defined by accessibility to the human in its entirety. If, as Alain says, one is capable of every vice and every virtue, but "according to the inimitable form of life that each man has for a law," the idea of man is presupposed in positing the individuality of each one. If character is not to be a thing or a static portrait seen from the outside, it must be a perspective on humanity. Human likeness is implied in the mutual otherness of individual characters.

20. *Etants* for Heidegger's *Seiendes* [Trans.].

But I do not think of the pole opposed to character, i.e., the pole of happiness, otherwise than as the ultimate end of man's function. I could not form the idea of happiness if I did not form that of a destination, of a human assignation, which as we saw is governed by the demand for totality. Because man demands the totality of meaning, his desire is directed toward happiness as a totality of meaning and contentment.

If I think character and happiness only *on* the idea of man, then what do I think in thinking man? A certain form, to be sure. But a form that calls for a "synthesis" at the outset.

What synthesis is this? We recall that objectivity was nothing but the expectation of a reality that was at once susceptible of appearing while affecting me in my receptivity and of letting itself be determined by articulate speech. In the form of the person, I intend a synthesis of a new kind: that of an end of my action which would be, at the same time, an existence. An end, consequently a goal to which all the means and calculations of means are subordinate; or, in other words, an end in itself, that is, one whose value is not subordinated to anything else; and at the same time an existence that one apprehends, or, to be more precise, a presence with which one enters into relations of mutual understanding, exchange, work, sociality.

Kant's remarks are very instructive in this connection, and more especially since he did not particularly consider the symmetry between the synthesis of the thing and the synthesis of the person. The reason, of course, is because he was so preoccupied with reducing the person to a simple "example" of the law (we shall later see what brings about our concern for extricating the constitution of the person from the sphere of morality). Kant says that "rational beings are designated 'persons' because their nature indicates that they are ends in themselves. . . . Man and, in general, every rational being exists as an end in himself and not merely as a means to be arbitrarily used by this or that will."[21] In a still more striking expression, whose brevity clearly brings out the "synthetic" constitution of the person, the person is "an existence having in itself an absolute worth"; or again, "an objective end, i.e., a being whose existence in itself is an end." It is this synthesis of reason and existence in the idea of an

21. *Foundations of the Metaphysics of Morals*, trans. Beck, p. 86.

end in itself that Kant states in the least approximative proposition of all those that we just enumerated: "Rational nature exists as an end in itself."[22]

Thus the Self, the Self as a person, is given first in an intention. In positing the person as an existing end, consciousness becomes self-consciousness. This self is still a projected self, as the thing was the project of what we called "consciousness." Self-consciousness is, like the consciousness of the thing, an intentional consciousness. But whereas the intending of the thing was a theoretical intention, the intending of the person is a practical intention; it is not yet an experienced plentitude but an "is to be"; the person is an "is to be," and the only way to achieve it is to "make it be." In Kantian terminology, the person is a way of treating others and of treating oneself. That is why Kant formulates the imperative in these terms: "Act so that you treat humanity, whether in your own person or in that of another, always as an end and never as a means only."[23] Humanity is a way of treating men, you as well as me. It is neither you nor I, it is the practical ideal of the "Self" in you as well as in me.

If, then, the person is primarily the ideal of the person, and, to be more precise, the "synthesis" of reason and existence, of end and of presence, it should be possible to go back from this idea to the experience in which it is constituted.

The synthesis of the person is constituted in a specific moral feeling, what Kant called respect. Thus there is a striking resemblance between the position of respect in Kant's practical philosophy and that of transcendental imagination in the theoretical philosophy. The synthesis of the object comes from the transcendental imagination; the two poles of understanding and receptivity meet in the transcendental imagination. Likewise, the synthesis of the person as an ethical object comes out of respect. We shall see of what "disproportion" respect is the fragile, subjective synthesis.

Let us therefore pursue the Kantian notion of respect, reserving the right to enlarge afterward on the narrowly moral perspective of his analysis.[24]

22. Ibid.
23. Ibid., p. 87.
24. I am fully aware here of changing the gist of the Kantian analysis of respect. For Kant respect is respect for law, and the person is only one example of it. Consequently, I am using Kantianism freely by putting respect

Just as the transcendental imagination was the third term homogeneous with both understanding and sensibility, so also *respect* is a paradoxical "intermediary" that belongs both to sensibility, that is, to the faculty of desiring, and to reason, that is, to the power of obligation that comes from practical reason. Imagination was the condition of the synthesis in the object; respect is the condition of the synthesis in the person.

Paradoxical intermediary, indeed: for we could say of respect, with more justice than of the transcendental imagination, "that it remains an art concealed in the depths of the human soul. . . ." Clear in its object, the person's humanity, respect is in itself the obscure thing that Kant calls an *a priori* incentive of which we can speak only by drawing together opposed terms without showing its true unity. After having shown that pure reason is practical only if it excludes the faculty of desiring—"pure reason is practical of itself alone and it gives [to man] a universal law, which we call the *moral law*;"[25] "not only . . . pure reason can be practical but . . . it alone

and person in a direct relation of intentionality. However, in betraying Kantian orthodoxy, I think I bring out the Kantian philosophy of the person that is outlined in the *Foundations* and stifled in the *Critique of Practical Reason*, the latter being wholly devoted to the elucidation of the synthesis of will and law in autonomy. The *Foundations* outlines a development that can hardly be reduced to the mere search for a foundation for autonomy; it aims at restoring a certain plenitude to moral reflection, moving in a direction opposed to that of the formalization that was necessary to the elaboration of the pure formal imperative. That search for plentitude is answered by the successive formulations of the categorical imperative. In turn, those formulations draw upon the ideas of nature, person, and kingdom. Kant himself proposes the idea that all that is there is not the mere illustration of the formal rule, but the possible counterpart to formalism: "All maxims have: (1) a form, which consists in universality . . . (2) a material, i.e., an end . . . (3) a complete determination of all maxims by this formula. . . . There is a progression here like that through the categories of the unity of the form of the will (its universality), to the plurality of material (the objects, i.e., the ends), to the totality or integrity of the system" (*Foundations*, Beck pp. 93–94). Kant limits the above by granting that this progression serves only to bring reason closer to intuition and therefore to feeling. But this valuable note bids us to consider the philosophy of the person not as an illustration but as the passage from "form" to "matter" and toward the complete "characterization" of all maxims that is attained only with the idea of a kingdom of ends.

25. *Critique of Practical Reason*, Beck p. 143.

and not the empirically conditioned reason is unconditionally prac-tical"[26]—we must establish that reason is practical only if it "in-fluences" the faculty of desiring.

We can see why: if reason were only a "principle" and not an "incentive," it would allow us to judge, appreciate or condemn, but it would not move to action; it would be not practical but only critical in the moral sense of the word. Accordingly, it is necessary that law come down into the very maxim of action, that is, touch the heart of free choice, which is not immediately convinced by the law, but, according to the *Foundations*, "stands, as it were, at the cross-roads halfway between its *a priori* principle which is formal and its *a posteriori* incentive which is material."[27] The principle will be practical only if duty moves the will. That is why the "principle" must become an "incentive"—if by incentive we understand "a sub-jective determining ground of a will whose reason does not by its nature necessarily conform to the objective law."[28]

Thus the enigma of respect is indeed that of the practical synthesis of reason and finitude, therefore that of the third term. On the one hand, reason "influences" the faculty of desiring: it is therefore necessary to forge the idea of an *a priori* feeling, that is, one pro-duced by reason, reason becoming an "incentive to make this law itself a maxim."[29] On the other hand, sensibility is made accessible to reason. If this "access" is experienced as a constraint, a violence upon the subdued desire, nothing could be more natural in the frame-work of downfall that the moralist presupposes, and the Kantian analysis strongly emphasized the negative aspects of this influence. The important thing is that through this emotion of subdued desire the faculty of desiring is "elevated" to the level of reason, and that in this way self-esteem is born in the heart of this finitude elevated to reason. This esteem attests that the law "finds entrance into the mind."[30]

The paradoxical constitution of "respect," like that of the tran-scendental imagination, is such that this feeling upon which the practical synthesis rests cannot be reflected without being destroyed.

26. Ibid., p. 129.
27. *Foundations*, Beck p. 61.
28. *Critique of Practical Reason*, Beck p. 180.
29. Ibid., p. 184.
30. Ibid., p. 193.

In respect I am an obeying subject *and* a commanding sovereign; but I cannot imagine this situation otherwise than as a twofold mode of *belonging*, "so that the person as belonging to the world of sense is subject to his own personality so far as he belongs to the intelligible world."[31] Into this twofold belonging is written the possibility of a discord and what is, as it were, the existential "fault"[32] that causes man's fragility.

This analysis of the fragile experience in which the notion of person is constituted has been conducted with the resources of Kantian ethics. One may entertain reservations with regard to Kantianism, especially concerning the relation between the person and the law, but these reservations do not radically change the ethical aspect of the analysis. On the other hand, one might object that this analysis does not suit an anthropology of fallibility because it flows from a pessimistic anthropology dominated by the theory of *radical evil*. In the analysis of respect, the Kantian moralist presupposes an *already* fallen sensibility, and it is this that he excludes from the moral sphere. Thus, adopting a moral philosophy that moves in the dimension of downfall for an anthropology of fallibility would make a vicious circle inevitable. We must push the objection even further and challenge the value, for the kind of investigations we are here pursuing, of any anthropology linked to an ethical vision of the world. The moralist starts with a situation in which the duality of good and evil is already constituted, in which man has already chosen the side of evil. All the moral problems of reconciliation, peace, and unity pose themselves in the wake of such a situation of war between man and man, between man and himself.

The objection is strong, and we cannot be content with answering that Kant does not situate evil in sensibility as such, but in a maxim of the will that reverses the order of the pre-eminence of law and sensibility. For in an ethical vision of the world, such a choice for the bad has already been committed, and sensibility, without itself being the principle of evil, turns toward the moralist a countenance disfigured by the passions of greed, power, and glory. Thenceforward, the analysis of respect is crushed by the dualism of Logos and Pathos, which every theory of the "passions" imposes.

Nor is it enough to answer that Kant does not bracket sensibility

31. Ibid.
32. *Faille*, fault in geological sense [Trans.].

considered as evil but as empirical, that it is critical rigor and not
moral rigorism that requires its exclusion.

Certainly this purely "methodological" interpretation of the exclusion of the faculty of desiring from the sphere of morality is very
valuable. But it is only suitable for the first phase of the critique
of *Practical Reason*, the one that is devoted to the establishment of
the "principle" of morality, that is, of the determining power of
practical reason over the will in a rational being in general. It is
no longer of value in the search for the "incentive," which presupposes finite reason rather than reason in general and at the same
time refers to a rebellious sensibility. This comes out in the analysis
devoted to the effects of the law on the faculty of desiring. In Kant the
negative effects prevail over the positive effects: law "elevates" "sensibility" only by "subduing" it. Indeed, what is presupposed here is a
fallen sensibility. We must, then, take the objection in its radicality
as an objection of principle directed not only against Kant but against
any ethical vision of the world.

We can only answer this: We have access to the primordial only
through what is fallen. In return, if the fallen denotes nothing about
that *from which* it has fallen, no philosophy of the primordial is
possible, and we cannot even say that man is fallen. For the very
idea of downfall involves reference to the loss of a certain innocence
that we understand sufficiently to name it and to designate the present
condition as a lapse, a loss or a fall. I cannot understand treason as
evil without judging it by an idea of trust and loyalty in relation to
which it is evil.

Thus, from the methodological point of view the situation is not
hopeless. We have only to keep in mind that it is through a dualism,
which flows from an ethical vision of the world as fallen and of man
as *already* divided against himself, that we must decipher and interpret the initial "disproportion" which underlies and dis-tends man's
practical existence.

The problem could be stated in these terms: to rediscover, through
the consideration of an ethical dualism and prior to its condem-
nation of sensibility, the structure of fallibility that has made this
dualism possible. Such a regression could be called a reconquest of
the primordial "practical" dimension over its derivative dualist and
"ethical" aspect. Is this movement from the "ethical" duality to the
"practical" disproportion possible?

Not only is the movement possible, but it is necessary to the intelligibility of the "ethical" dualism. We find in Kant himself the beginnings of this retrogressive movement which we shall soon have to pursue without him.

Indeed, how could law "subject" sensibility, "humiliate" its presumption, if it did not have "access" to it? The root of this constraint, the origin of this humiliation, is a pure determination of sensibility by reason, a taking over of the faculty of desiring by rationality, which raises it above mere nature. The relationship of respect with admiration and the sublime provides here a decisive "analogy." Try as he may to distinguish respect and admiration, Kant yields to something like admiration when he exclaims, rather like Rousseau: "Duty! Thou sublime and mighty. . . ." Respect is therefore rooted in something like a disposition of desire for rationality, like the Cartesian generosity that is at once action and passion, action of the free will and emotion in the depths of the body. Another example is the Platonic Eros who suffers from and rejoices over his relationship with the metempirical world. Indeed, in the economy of downfall, which is also that of ethics, respect cannot resorb its negative aspect of coercion into its positive aspect of aspiration. But coercion and aspiration are not on the same level: coercion is the psychological wrapping, the experienced appearance; aspiration is the anthropological root. That is why the "Methodology of Practical Reason," which takes the point of view of the "access" of the laws of reason to the *Gemüt*, of their influence on the maxims of this mind, begins to go beyond the ethical dualism toward a more radical anthropology symbolized by the term *Gemüt*. The *Gemüt* is that region in which reason, the representation of duty, has an immediate "force" and is capable by itself of taking "preference." "If human nature were not so constituted [*geschaffen*], no way of presenting the law by circumlocutions and indirect recommendations could ever produce morality of intentions."[33] This recourse to a constitution of human nature brings to the fore the "property of our *Gemüt*," namely, "this receptivity [*Empfändlichkeit*] to a pure moral interest."[34] This capacity to undergo the influence of the moral incentive is the root we are trying to uncover. But it is a theory of the *Gemüt* that is required and no longer merely a theory of finite reason. Kant evokes

33. *Critique of Practical Reason,* Beck p. 244.
34. Ibid., p. 250.

this theory in the famous apostrophe in the *Critique*: "Two things fill the mind [*Gemüth*] with ever new and increasing admiration and awe, the oftener and more steadily they are reflected on: the starry heavens above me and the moral law within me."[35] Admiration and awe are beyond and before a violated sensibility of subdued presumption. They witness the affinity of sensibility for rationality. Now, Kant continues, "I do not merely conjecture them and seek them as though obscured in darkness or in the transcendent region beyond my horizon: I see them before me, and I associate them directly with the consciousness of my own existence."[36] This *Gemüt*, called the consciousness of my existence, is nothing other than the positive relation which we are looking for of desire to the moral law and which Kant calls elsewhere the "destination," purpose, or assignation (*Bestimmung*) of man, which "infinitely raises my worth." Such is the root of respect: it flows "from the purposive destination assigned to my existence by this law"[37] (*aus der zweckmässigen Bestimmung meines Daseins durch dieses Gesetz*).

Kantianism, however, abandons us here. Its *Anthropology* is in no way an exploration of the primordial. It is a description of man in the perspective of the "passions" and an ethical dualism.

The only way to continue toward this *Gemüt*, which would be the "practical" substructure of the "ethical" dualism, is to situate the inner duality of respect in the extension of the duality of *perspective* and *verb*, which owes nothing to the consideration of a fallen sensibility or a radical evil. In fact, the objectivity that has served as a reference pole to this reflective investigation is neither innocent nor guilty. It is neutral with respect to the problematic of radical evil. Unlike ethical reflection dominated by the clash of good and evil, of value and non-value, and by the description of man as having already chosen evil, transcendental reflection presupposes no opposition to objectivity, no resistance of sensibility to reason. For it, objectivity is not value, a polar opposite to non-value; it is merely the "natural light" in which something can appear and sustain determination. In short, transcendental reflection is on the primordial level at the very outset. It does not have to reach it through a depraved condition. That is why it has been able to serve as a guide for

35. Ibid.
36. Ibid., p. 258.
37. Ibid., p. 259.

the exploration of the "practical" disproportion that is more primal than the ethical duality, and *to uncover a principle of limitation that would not already be radical evil.*

Our previous investigation of character and happiness was already replying to this requirement: the "practical" polarity of character and happiness constitutes the anthropological root of any "ethical" dualism. That polarity does not presuppose downfall: all the aspects of finitude have been regrouped under the idea of finite perspective; all the aspects of infinitude have been regrouped under the idea of Meaning or Verb. Thus, we can already say that respect is the fragile synthesis in which the form of the person is constituted, just as the transcendental imagination was the hidden synthesis in which the thing's form is constituted.

It remains for us to prolong this constitution of the "practical" moment of respect by the development of its "affective" moment; in short, to reveal the texture of *Gemüt,* of *feeling* as such.

4

Affective Fragility

THIS REFLECTIVE ANALYSIS started from the thing in front of me and the person conceived as the ideal of the self. What does our analysis lack in order to be equal to the understanding of man that was anticipated in the myths and rhetoric of misery? What is missing in such a reflection is the dimension of feeling.

Indeed, the understanding of "misery" from which we started was a pathetic understanding. Is it possible to salvage this *pathétique* for philosophy? At first we had to turn away from it, exorcise it, reduce it: it was the work of transcendental reflection to break off with the *pathétique* and to take the thing and the person for reflective references.

The virtue in formalism was in transforming what was at first only an immense and confused emotion into a philosophic problem. But what has been gained in rigor has been lost in richness and depth. Is it possible to win back that plentitude by beginning with this rigor? Is it possible to understand feeling beginning with what reduced it and excluded it?

This question of method conceals another question that concerns the substance of the problem: if a philosophy of feeling is possible, how can it be related to an investigation of human fallibility? What more is there in the *feeling* of the self than in the project of the object in which consciousness in general is constituted? What more is there in feeling than in the project of the person in which self-consciousness determines itself? After consciousness and self-consciousness, what step could possibly appear that would reveal a new sense of human disproportion?

"Disproportion," we saw, was apprehended only *on* the objectivity of the thing, *on* the humanity of the person: do we finally, with feeling, have the moment in which disproportion becomes for itself? Here we encounter Plato's valuable idea on the θυμός, the median function *par excellence* in the human soul. The θυμός is the living

transition from βίος (life) to λόγος. At one and the same time it
separates and unites vital affectivity or desire (ἐπιθυμία) and the
spiritual affectivity that the *Symposium* calls ἔρως. In the *Republic*,
Plato says that the θυμός sometimes battles on the side of reason, in
the form of energy and courage; sometimes it enters the service of
desire as an enterprising power, as irritation and anger. Can a modern
theory of feeling come back to that intuition of Plato?

If that is possible, the third step of an anthropology of fallibility
is the "heart," the *Gemüt*, Feeling. In advancing step by step from
consciousness in general to self-consciousness and then to feeling,
or, in other words, from the theoretical to the practical to the affective, philosophical anthropology would progress toward a point that
is at once more inward and more fragile. The moment of the fragility
of consciousness in general was, we recall, the transcendental imagination that was both intellectual and sensible. But the transcendental
imagination, a blind point of knowledge, transcended itself intentionally in its correlate, the thing. Consequently the synthesis of speech
and appearance is a synthesis in the thing itself, or rather in the objectivity of the thing.

The second moment of fragility was that of respect. It corre-
sponded to the project of the self or the person. But the paradoxical,
disproportionate constitution of respect was transcended intentionally in the representation of the person, which was still a kind of
objective or objectival synthesis.

The "heart," the restless heart, would be the fragile moment *par
excellence*. All the disproportions that we have seen culminate in the
disproportion of happiness and character would be interiorized in
the heart.

But the question is whether a philosophy of the "heart" is possible. It must be a philosophy which is not a relapse into the *pathétique*, but which is brought to the level of reason—in the literal sense
of the word level—to the level of that reason which is not satisfied
with the pure and the radical, but which demands the total, the
concrete.

The direction in which we must look is shown to us by the very
movement of the preceding reflection. That reflection was made up
of a reduction of the *pathétique*. But that *pathétique* was not devoid
of all thematic structure; it was not utterly alien to the sphere of
speech for it even had a language proper to it, that of myth and

rhetoric. Therefore, if that pathos was already mythos, that is, speech, it must be possible to reconstruct it in the dimension of philosophic discourse. Now, this mythos bespoke the primordial crucifixion that is the misery of the intermediate being. A merely transcendental reflection of the thing has not fully restored that theme, nor has the practical reflection on the person. If a philosophy of feeling is possible, it is feeling that should express the fragility of the intermediate being that we are. In other words, what is at stake in a philosophy of feeling is the very gap between the purely transcendental exegesis of "disproportion" and the lived experience of "misery."

The two questions are connected, the question of method and the question of substance: the question of the possibility of a philosophy of feeling and that of a completion of the meditation on "disproportion" in the dimension of feeling. We must resolve these two questions together.

INTENTIONALITY AND INWARDNESS OF FEELING

A reflection on the universal function of feeling in relation to knowing should suffice to establish the possibility of the culminating of anthropology in a philosophy of feeling. Indeed, the significance of feeling appears in the reciprocal genesis of knowing and feeling. Taken outside of this mutual genesis, feeling is no more than a word that covers a host of partial functions: affective regulations, disturbing emotions, affective states, vague intuitions, passions, etc. Put back into the movement of their mutual promotion, feeling and knowing "explain each other." On the one hand, the power of knowing, by hierarchizing itself, truly engenders the *degrees* of feeling and pulls it out of its essential confusion. On the other hand, feeling indeed generates the *intention* of knowing on all its levels. The unity of *sentir*, of *Fühlen*, of feeling, is constituted in this mutual genesis.

The reciprocity of feeling and knowing may be established by means of a rather simple intentional analysis. Disregarding for the moment the difference of *level* of the feelings in question and considering only the "horizontal" relation that feeling sets up between the self and the world, we may ask ourselves what the meaning of the relation between love and the lovable, between hate and the hateful is. This relation that we call "horizontal" is necessarily very abstract since it neglects the difference in level of the very realities that feeling and knowing designate: love of the thing, love of the person, of values, of being, etc. But this abstraction is favorable to a pre-liminary investigation of the intentional structure that constitutes the unity of all the modes of feeling.

It is noteworthy that this analysis debouches straightway on an "aporia." Feeling, for instance love or hate, is without any doubt intentional: it is a feeling of "something"—the lovable, the hateful. But it is a very strange intentionality that on the one hand designates qualities felt *on* things, *on* persons, *on* the world, and on the other hand manifests and reveals the way in which the self is inwardly affected. This paradox is quite perplexing: an intention and an af-fection coincide in the same experience, a transcending aim and the revelation of an inwardness. Moreover, in bearing on qualities felt *on the world*, feeling manifests an affectively-moved self. The *af-fective* aspect of feeling vanishes as soon as its intentional aspect fades away, or it at least sinks into an inexpressible obscurity. It is only thanks to its aim, overspilling itself into a felt quality, into an affective "correlate," that feeling can be expressed, said, communi-cated, and worked out in a cultural language. Our "affections" are read on the world they develop, which reflects their kinds and nuances.

We cannot void the intentional moment of feeling, therefore, with-out at the same time voiding the affective moment of the self. And yet on the other hand we hesitate, and rightly so, to call these corre-lates of feeling *objects*. The hateful and the lovable are "meant" *on* things but do not have the peculiar subsistence of objects the obser-vation of which one can never complete. They are only qualities that must be "founded" on the perceived and known objects in order to appear in the world. The nature of these intentional correlates is such that they cannot be separated from the representative moments of the thing; they are intentional correlates but without autonomy. It is the perceived and known object that endows them with a center of significance, a pole of objectivity, and, one might say, the sub-stantive of reality. The hateful and the lovable by themselves are only floating qualifiers; they are not "in" consciousness, to be sure, since they are the intended and the signified. But, for that matter, the moment of exteriority does not belong to them: it belongs to the percept as such. It is the percept that implies the fundamental extension by which things are placed outside of us and, it might be said, outside of themselves, spread out and manifested by the exteriority and the mutual exclusion of the parts. For this reason, we need the help of an observed thing or a present person in order to bring the lovable and the hateful into the light of the world.

What is lacking to the felt as such, and what is still more basic than the moment of exteriority, is the positional moment, the natural belief in existence: it is the property of perception to signify a thing that is, a "being,"[1] by means of sensorial qualities—colors, sounds, tastes, etc. Feeling is not positional in this sense; it does not believe in the being of what it aims at, it does not posit any "being." And it is because it does not posit any "being" that it manifests the way in which I am affected, *my* love and *my* hate, although it manifests it only through the lovable and the hateful, meant on the thing, on the person, and on the world.

This is the paradox of feeling. How can the same experience *designate* a thing-quality and, through this thing-quality, manifest, express, and reveal the inwardness of an I?

Here the reciprocity of feeling and knowing is very illuminating. Knowing, because it exteriorizes and poses its object in being, sets up a fundamental cleavage between the object and the subject. It "detaches" the object or "opposes it" to the I. In short, knowing constitutes the duality of subject and object. Feeling is understood, by contrast, as the manifestation of a relation to the world that constantly restores our complicity with it, our inherence and belonging in it, something more profound than all polarity and duality.[2]

This relation to the world, which is irreducible to any *objectival* polarity, can be certainly named but not recaptured in itself. We can name it ante-predicative, pre-reflective, pre-objective, or hyper-predicative, hyper-reflective, hyper-objective as well. But because we live in the subject–object duality that has structured our language, this relation can be reached only *indirectly*.

We can progress in our understanding of feeling, conceived as the counterpart of objectification, in the following way: Feeling is the privileged mode through which this pre- and hyper-objective relation is revealed. But it is not the only one. What behavioristic psychology

1. *Etant* [Trans.].
2. W. Stern, *Allgemeine Psychologie auf personalistischer Grundlage* (The Hague, 1950). S. Strasser, *Das Gemüt* (Freiburg, 1956).

calls tendencies, tensions, and drives is that same relation to the world, but expressed in terms of action and reaction. To understand the relation between feeling and tendency is to understand at the same time the relation to the world that is expressed in these two broken languages, that of behavior and that of experience. If it were understood that the objective direction of a behavior and the aim of a feeling are one and the same thing, that feeling is nothing but the very direction of behavior as felt, we would understand both tendency and feeling, and, in understanding them, one by the other, we would advance in our understanding of the still more fundamental reciprocity of feeling and knowing.

The very intentionality of tendencies is what feeling manifests through affective tones meant *on* things. The very things "toward which" our desires approach, "far from which" they withdraw, "against which" they fight are the lovable, the hateful, the easy, and the difficult.

This thesis is the cornerstone of our whole reflection and deserves more elucidation. The privileged position of a revealer that we give to feeling, with regard to the *élans* of our being and with regard to its pre- and hyper-objective connections with the beings of the world, encounters two kinds of oppositions: that of behavioristic psychology and that of depth psychology.

The first would maintain that what is "experienced" constitutes only the conscious region of behavior, only a fragment of behavior, and that it is the whole of behavior that develops a complete sense and thus confers a partial sense on its silent phases as well as on its conscious phases. To this we must reply that feeling is not a part of a whole, but a significant moment of the whole. The affective experience manifests the meaning of wanting . . . , tending toward . . . , attaining . . . , possessing, and enjoying. Behavioristic psychology, indeed, is condemned to work with metaphorical notions, such as equilibrium, maladjustment, tension, resolution of tension. These metaphors are useful: they bring about well-conducted experiments, regroup empirical results into a coherent view; in short, they are good working concepts. But what is the meaning of these metaphors borrowed from another "region" of reality, that of the physical thing? What are they the metaphors of? Behavioristic psychology can dodge the question as long as the purport of its concepts is of less consequence than their experimental yield. But as soon as the question "What do drive and tension mean?" is raised, we must resort to another kind of investigation and note that tensions and drives have a psychological turn, and therefore differ from the physical model of which they are the analogue, only in consequence of the remarkable property of anticipating their resolution in an intentional way. A physical tension does not encompass its final equilibrium in anticipation; the end is not intentionally present in its beginning and in its development. It is here that an intentional analysis relieves the "energy" metaphor and saves it as a metaphor. The psychologist can and should continue to speak in terms of drives, but he does not know what he is saying. Or rather he knows what he is saying thanks to the implicit intentional analysis that quietly reminds him that his use of "energy" language is only metaphorical.

Feeling, therefore, is nothing other than the manifestation of the implicit intention of "tensions" and "drives." Not only is the manifestation of the intention of tensions by feeling the only thing that can save the physical metaphor as a metaphor of the psychic, but it alone can justify the "regulative" role that behavioristic psychology recognizes in feeling: for in exhibiting the aim of the tendency on the predicates of things, feeling can furnish to action the objective signals by which it can regulate itself. Feeling "serves" the tendency by "expressing" it on an outside, by projecting valences on the very appearance of the world. That which appears to us as a quality, there, on the thing, is the manifestation of the moment, the phase, the state of the tendency. By means of this manifestation the tendency tells where it is: wanting, under way, satisfied. Thus intentional analysis, far from being an alternative to behavioristic psychology, is the full justification of it: the whole effort of psychology to work out a coherent concept of "motivation," to give a functional significance or a regulative role to feeling in relation to action, finds in the reflection on intentional signification an explication and a foundation.

But depth psychology objects that experienced feeling merely gives the apparent sense of life and that it is necessary to decipher, by means of a special heremeneutics, the latent meaning that is also the real meaning, whose manifest meaning is nothing but a symptom. Feeling is the locus of all masks, dissimulations, and mystifications. Were we not aware of this before Freud through La Rochefoucauld and Nietzsche? Indeed we were. But this observation does not show up the weakness of feeling but confirms that feeling *manifests* tendencies; for dissimulation is still an aspect of the manifestation. Indeed, as far as we can and should go on the road of suspicion concerning the apparent sense, it is nevertheless that which introduces drives into the dimension of the signifying. Feeling is the revealer of intentionality; whether or not this revealer is dissimulating is a further complication that takes nothing away from the fundamental yield of the manifestation that binds "the acted" to "the felt." That is why the latent meaning could be only an exegesis of the apparent meaning, a search for a better meaning. Non-sense or the senseless is still within the dimension of sense in which feeling moves. The hermeneutics of meaning always moves from the least to the most meaningful sense. And the psychotherapist, in initiating this exegesis of meaning, has no other goal than to make a new meaning acceptable which will be lived in a more authentic way and which will manifest more veridically the intentional reality of life.

We may now embrace the whole range of the dialectic of feeling and knowing. While we oppose ourselves to objects by means of the representation, feeling attests our coaptation, our elective harmonies and disharmonies with realities whose affective image we carry in ourselves in the form of "good" and "bad." The Scholastics had an excellent word to express this mutual coaptation of man to goods that suit him and to bads that do not. They spoke of a bond of connaturality between my being and other beings. This bond of connaturality is silently effected in our tendential life; we feel it in a conscious and sensory way in all our affections, but we do not understand it in reflection except by contrast with the movement of objectification proper to knowing. Consequently feeling can be defined only by this very contrast between the movement by means of which we "detach" over against us and "objectify" things and beings, and the movement by means of which we somehow "appropriate" and interiorize them.

We can see why feeling, thus intermingled with the adventure of knowledge and objectivity, must present to reflection the paradoxical intentional texture that we described. For it is *on* the things elaborated by the work of objectification that feeling projects its affective correlates, its felt qualities: the lovable and the hateful, the desirable and the loathsome, the sad and the joyous; thus it seems to play the game of the object. But since these qualities are not objects facing a subject but the intentional expression of an undivided bond with the world, feeling appears at the same time as a coloring of the soul, as an affection: it is this landscape which is cheerful, and it is I who am elated. Feeling expresses my belonging to this landscape that, in turn, is the sign and cipher of my inwardness. Now, since the whole of our language has been worked out in the dimension of objectivity, in which the subject and object are distinct and opposed, feeling can be described only paradoxically as the unity of an intention and an affection, of an intention toward the world and an affection of the self. This paradox, however, is only the sign pointing toward the mystery of feeling, namely, the undivided connection of my existence with beings and being through desire and love.

We betray this unity of intention and affection as soon as we allow ourselves to be taken in by the language of objectivity in which we are condemned to express it. And we can be mistaken in two ways.

Not finding in feeling the mode of objectivity proper to the thing, we say it is "subjective." In that case we miss its intentional dimension and falsify the connection between the objectivity of knowing and the intentionality peculiar to feeling. This intentionality cannot be reduced to a centripetal movement opposed to the centrifugal movement of observation, knowing, and willing; feeling is also centrifugal inasmuch as it manifests the aim of feelings. And it is only insofar as it manifests this aim that it manifests myself as affected. It is at the price of these explicit reservations that one can make depth the dimension proper to feeling. This depth is not the contrary of intentionality but the contrary of the objectification peculiar to representation: whereas representation sets at a distance and, even in exploratory touching, "detaches" the signified unities to which it relates the impressions of touch, feeling brings closer. By means of feeling, objects touch me. Objects that are imperfectly objective make contact; unauthentic feelings remain superficial. True objects are at a distance, and true feelings are profound; they reach us, sometimes transfix us, as with the deep-seated wound of a great mourning.

Conversely, out of a concern for doing justice to the specific intentionality of feeling, we attribute to feeling objects or quasi-objects that we shall call *values*. We have taken a risk, it is true, in speaking earlier of "valence," as certain contemporary psychologists do, and in calling "good" and "bad," along with the Scholastics and Descartes, the intentional correlate of love and hate, the fitting and the unfitting, the familiar and the alien, the kindred and the hostile upon which our actions are patterned. Indeed, feelings vary following the absence, distance, and presence of these "valences," of this "good" and that "bad." Love and hate, desire, hope and despair, fear and boldness may be distinguished, said Descartes, "because of the diverse ways in which they [the objects that move the senses] may harm or help us, or in general be of some importance."[3] Our intentional analysis enables us to go as far as the epithets of good and bad, of the suitable and the harmful (even as far as the substantive epithets of valence, importance, harm), but no further. The introduction of the notion of value brings into play two operations that go beyond our present analysis, and we shall not express an opinion on these for the moment: value can be spoken of only following a "reduction" executed precisely on the "good" and the "bad," therefore on goods, valences, and harms, in the sense we just indicated. This reduction, which may well be called an eidetic reduction, consists in bracketing the valence of the thing so as to bring before the mind the essence that is the *a priori* of the good and the bad here and now. Furthermore, these essences merit the name of value only when referred to each other and seized in an order of preference; this *a priori* preference reveals the valences as values by bestowing a relative worth on them. With regard to an *ordo amoris*, this reduction to essence and this preferential intuition are the two conditions which give one the right to speak of value. Now, these are acts of the mind, undoubtedly one and the same act of the mind, one and the same intuition, at once essential and preferential, which it is not fitting to call feeling but preferential intuition, if we wish to respect its particular nature: the pleasant and the unpleasant, met with on things, are not yet values; they become so only when they are reduced to essence and confronted with other values in a preferential outlook. Without this reduction and this preferential outlook, feeling aims only at "goods" and "bads." These false substantives still point only to the intentional signs of our affections.

3. *The Passions of the Soul*, art. 52.

"HOMO SIMPLEX IN VITALITATE, DUPLEX IN HUMANITATE"

If feeling manifests what life aims at, if it reveals the orientation of tendencies that direct our lives toward the world, feeling must *add* a new dimension to the merely transcendental understanding of human reality. Furthermore, if feeling manifests its meaning only by contrast with the work of objectification proper to knowing, if its general function is to interiorize the reality that we objectify over against us, then the advent of feeling is necessarily contemporary with that of knowledge. And we see from this that the disproportion of knowing may both be reflected and reach its completion in that of feeling.

A joint reflection on knowing and feeling therefore leads us to the central theme of this meditation, namely, that feeling divides in two, *like* knowing, proportionately to knowing and yet *differently* from knowing in a non-objective way, in the mode of an inner conflict.

The genesis of feeling and knowing indeed has a double sense. On the one hand, the theory of the object introduces a principle of differentiation and hierarchy into affective confusion. It removes the indetermination and the abstraction of our previous analysis: in point of fact we were able to reflect on the relations between love and the lovable without specifying whether it was a question of things, persons, ideas, communities, or God. By interiorizing itself in feeling, the relation to the object is now going to set up rank among tendencies and differentiate feeling in its very inwardness. The first benefit of a mutual genesis of feeling and knowing is therefore to lead from a *horizontal* analysis of love and the lovable in general to a *vertical* analysis of the degrees of feeling in accordance with the degree of objects. In this way the full range of feeling and its inner disproportion will be brought to light.

Furthermore, the coming to awareness of this disproportion, which first lost itself in the object, reaches its completion in feeling. Ultimately, it is in the *life* of feeling that the intermediate "term" is reflected, the term of which we vainly tried to catch a live awareness in the "theoretical" and "practical" registers. Thus our whole reflection on disproportion comes to center itself on one point that is somehow the locus and the node of disproportion. It is this affective node which Plato called θυμός and tried to situate between ἐπιθυμία, sensuous desire, and reason, whose specific desire is ἔρως. Thus the inner conflict of human desire reaches its climax in θυμός. In this sense θυμός constitutes the human feeling *par excellence*.

Our path is therefore clear: First we will proceed to the extremes— ἐπιθυμία and ἔρως—in order to understand the range of feeling in light of the range of reason. Then we will come back to the middle term—θυμός—in order to reach an understanding of the whole of man's fragility through that of feeling.

The range and the "disproportion" of feeling, therefore, are primarily a continuation of those of knowing. Our whole reflection on the object has been organized around the theme of two intentions, the perspectival and the truth intentions. Man appeared to us as a being stretched between the this-here-now, the certainty of the living present, and the need to complete knowledge in the truth of the whole. By whatever name this primordial duality is called—opinion and science, intuition and understanding, certainty and truth, presence and sense—it forbids us to formulate a philosophy of perception prior to a philosophy of discourse and forces us to work them out together, one with the other, one by the other.

Now, the idea of a primordial "disproportion" of feeling, contemporaneous with that of knowing, runs head-on into a prejudice that affective psychology has inherited from the old *Treatises on the Passions,* from the Stoics to Descartes, passing through St. Thomas. These treatises are based on the idea that all the "affections" can be derived in a progressive order, from the simple to the complex, by starting from a small number of simple, elementary, or principal passions. Our whole previous reflection bids us on the contrary to repudiate this composition of complex feelings and to *start not with the simple, but with the dual*; not with the elementary, but with the polar. If one does not take into consideration the primordial disproportion of vital desire and intellectual love (or of spiritual joy), one entirely misses the specific nature of human affectivity. Man's humanity is not reached by adding one more stratum to the basic substratum of tendencies (and affective states) that are assumed to be common to animal and man. Man's humanity is that discrepancy in levels, that initial polarity, that divergence of affective tension between the extremities of which is placed the "heart."

That is the working hypothesis. How can we put it to the test? The test that we propose will consist in questioning the affections that *terminate* the movement of need, love, and desire. It can be shown, in fact, that there are two kinds of *terminations* of affective movements: one of them completes and perfects isolated, partial, finite acts, or processes. This is pleasure. It falls to the other one to be the perfection of the total work of man; this would be the termination of a destiny, of a destination or an existential project. This would be happiness, no longer the empty idea of happiness that up to now we have opposed to character, but the fullness of happiness or beatitude. Accordingly, what can best manifest the polarity of ἐπιθυμία and ἔρως is the inner discord of these two terminations, consummations, or *perfections*. For this duality of "ends" animates and rules the duality of "movements" and "appetites" and internally divides human desire.

It is possible to submit pleasure to the same critique as we applied to finite perspective when we were showing that perspective is recognized as such only in the truth-intention that transgresses it. The same holds true for pleasure. It is the other affective intention that reveals it as pleasure, as mere pleasure. This can be seen already in the doubling power of feeling: I can suffer from enjoying and rejoice in suffering. These second-degree feelings hierarchize affectivity and clearly show the power of feeling to relate itself to pleasure and to behave with regard to it. This affective doubling ushers in and begins a kind of immanent critique of the principle of pleasure, quietly worked upon by the principle of happiness. This critique is itself felt more than thought, something like a discontentment in mere pleasure that would not be the sign, promise, and guarantee of happiness.

Now, this affective critique is quite difficult to distinguish from a moral and moralizing criticism that dismisses pleasure as evil. We have here a trap that is easy to fall into. Yet what we must try to restore is a truly affective critique that is nothing other than the manifestation of the eclipse of pleasure by happiness. One finds the key to this critique only by placing oneself not before evil but before goodness, the *perfection* of pleasure, such as Aristotle extolled it in the *Ethics*. Happiness does not transcend the evil of pleasure but the very perfection of pleasure. Only in these terms can the *finitude* of pleasure, which is more primordial than any adventitious evil, be manifested.

We see, then, that Aristotle is here the right guide. He vigorously resisted the whole previous tradition that saw in pleasure a "genesis," a "process," an "unlimited" odyssey, and in the end the source of a kind of existential unhappiness. Pleasure is perfect because it perfects; it is not in process: "For it is indeed a whole, and at no time could one find a pleasure whose form would be completed if the pleasure lasts longer."[4]

Its perfection, however, is a finite one. It dwells only in the instant, precarious and perishable like the very goods whose possession pleasure manifests in enjoyment. Thus this perfection is a partial one that stands out against the horizon of destiny as a whole, and the primordial innocence of pleasure is a threatened innocence. The principle of this threat lies in the horizon-act structure. Human action aims both at a self-sufficient totality, which would give, which would be beatitude, the enjoyment of happiness, and at a finite realization in discrete acts, in "results" sanctioned by a consciousness of success or pleasure. The repose in pleasure threatens to bring the dynamism of activity to a standstill and screen the horizon of happiness.

The perfection of pleasure is finite in another sense. Pleasure puts the seal of its perfection on bodily life; the very example that Aristotle chose to establish his theory of pleasure-perfection—that of the pleasant sensation, or, to be more precise, the pleasure of seeing—attests that pleasure punctuates and ratifies my organic rootedness in the world. It magnifies the dilection with which I cherish the life that passes through me and this center of perspective that I am. Thus the very perfection of pleasure binds me to life, for it shows that living is not one activity in the midst of others but the existential condition of all others. In joyfully affirming the "live first," pleasure never stops suggesting the postponement of the "philosophize afterward." And yet pleasure is total as is happiness; it represents happiness in the instant; but it is precisely this compression of happiness into the instant that threatens to arrest the dynamism of acting in the celebration of *Living*.

The mistake of all philosophies that make pleasure as such an evil is in confusing this spontaneous and tendential attachment to living with a real, actual, and prior downfall. This finite perfec-

4. *Nicomachean Ethics* X, 1174a 16–17.

tion—in the twofold temporal and functional sense—is only the
threat of a closing or sealing off of the affective horizon. Evil requires
a specific act of preference. "The lack of self-restraint and intemperance," which Aristotle speaks of under the heading of "vices," are
not "passion" (πάθος) but action (πρᾶξις), and this action is committed "willingly" in the first case and deliberately in the second. In
order for pleasure to become a βίος, "a way of living," it is necessary
for the evil-doer to "prefer it to everything." Then he is driven and
dragged about: but it is he who gave in. The blindness that hides the
horizon of happiness from him and the constraint that hinders his will
from springing forth are his own doing. Correlative to that voluntary
downfall, I understand what a primordial enjoyment might be, one
that would be not the living tomb of the soul but the instantaneous
perfection of life.

The finitude of pleasure is so little a matter of primordial evil that
the affective critique that reveals happiness as its beyond is not merely
the negation of pleasure but its recovery and reaffirmation. It is striking that Aristotle hesitated between two "places" for his discourse
on pleasure and treated it first as a psychological preface to the
exegesis of the specific pair of virtue and vice, self-restraint and intemperance (Book VII), and secondly as the lowest degree of happiness (Book X). Pleasure is at once that which can arrest itself and
us on the level of mere living, and that which can be dialectized in
all the degrees of human action, finally merging with happiness,
which would yield perfect pleasure.

This dialectic is internal to pleasure itself and therefore not thrown
out into the darkness of the will to live and vital egoism. It may be
represented by the dialectic of the adjective and the substantive, of
the ἡδύ and the ἡδονή. The French language has lost the key to it
by translating ἡδύ by agréable and ἡδονή by plaisir. The agréable is
pleasure itself, the "pleasant,"[5] marking out the dialectic proper to
action. In the form of the pleasant, pleasure is hierarchized as is
action. Thus we see it become aesthetic in perceiving works of art,
interiorize itself in the remembrance of the past, make itself change-
able in the pleasure of expenditure and play, dynamize itself as the

5. The French agréable and plaisir are commonly rendered by "pleasant"
and "pleasure," and in this sense the English language has not lost the key
to the Greek terms [Trans.].

joy of learning and endeavoring, open itself to another in the pleasures of friendship. There is no reason not to call "pleasures" all these varieties of pleasure. Aristotle's golden rule, according to which pleasure is the perfection of activity without hindrance, constitutes the unity of all the degrees of pleasure: "Pleasure perfects activities and consequently the life to which one aspires."[6]

But the pleasant which is pure completion becomes substantivized in pleasure and falls back to its sensuous, bodily model: a static state of pleasure tends to weigh down the dynamics of activity and therefore also the dynamics of the pleasant. The static state flows subtly from the dynamizing effect of pleasure, namely, its power to relaunch an activity and increase it through the attraction of the pleasant. Aristotle noted before that the pleasure we take in one activity makes us ill-disposed for another: "The pleasure of hearing the flute destroys, for those who love it, the pleasure that discourse might give them."[7] And so by narrowing the field of disposition, it "destroys" other activities.[8] Thus the pleasant accompanies our activities and tends to promote action; but pleasure privileges one activity and tends to hinder action. Pleasures, therefore, react upon the activities which they stand for. The exclusion of pleasures leads to the exclusion of activities.

Because of this substantification of the pleasant into pleasure and the enclosure of the consciousness of happiness within the consciousness of result, the problematic of happiness must necessarily be restored at the price of a certain suspension of pleasure. Happiness could be rediscovered by unlimiting the adjective-pleasure, the pleasant; but it is necessary to break through the enclosure of substantive pleasure. That is why Aristotle does not build the idea of happiness directly on pleasure, not even on the pleasant, but goes back to the very principle of activity and its dynamism. Happiness is the "desirable in itself" and not "for the sake of something else."[9] The final intentionality of happiness is found in activity itself and not in its pleasant accompaniment. That is why a certain "suspension" of pleasure is necessary for the radical significance of happiness to be made clear and for pleasure itself to be reaffirmed.

6. *Nicomachean Ethics* X, 1175a 15.
7. Ibid. 1175b 6.
8. Ibid. 1175b 23.
9. Ibid. 1176b 4.

The suspension of pleasure aims at restoring the dynamism and the hierarchy of human action and ultimately at finding the *supremely pleasant*. Plato effectuated this in his celebrated debate with Callicles in the *Gorgias*. It was enough for Callicles to grant him the possibility of distinguishing "better" and "worse" pleasures (499b) for a critique of pleasure to be made possible and set on its way. A "τέλος [end] of all our acts"—the good—is implicitly introduced as a measure of value or at least as a principle, foundation, or requirement for a concrete measure, such as a way of living (βίος), the style of a "function of man" (500c). In this way the division of the good and the pleasant is the instrument of the differentiation of the pleasant itself. The pleasant as such is without any manifest order; it is under the sway of the "good" that "excellences" or ἀρεταί are ranked, if it is true that the ἀρετή of each thing consists in an "ordering or arrangement" and that "a certain order proper to each existing thing is what, by its presence, makes it good." Thus the idea of a "soul having order"[10] is the guide for a dialectic of the affective.

The Greek theory of "virtue" has no other intention than that of restoring the primordial amplitude of the pleasant, through "suspension" of pleasure. Thus, it makes the pleasant or adjectival pleasure equal to happiness itself. The brilliant page of the *Gorgias* where Plato progressively constructs the notions of "good," "excellence" and "order," and then by means of the "suitable" rediscovers the chain of classical "virtues" of Greek παιδεία—temperance, wisdom, justice, piety, courage—starts the whole series of Treatises on Virtues up to modern times. "Virtue," taken in its first meaning of excellence, is the critical concept that supports the intentional aim of activity as a whole. In designating and distinguishing the multiple and collective excellences of action, the "virtues" reorient activity toward its lasting and final totality. Particularly temperance, which directly concerns the good use of pleasure, gives activity its flexibility and openness; temperance is the "practical" ἐποχή of pleasure, thanks to which the dynamism of preference is put back into movement. Whoever is master of his pleasures is free in his actions and open to happiness. That is the meaning of the saying that moral preaching has rendered so banal: "Happiness lies in virtuous activities."[11] Indeed, considered in its most radical intention, the critique

10. *Gorgias* 506d–e.
11. *Nicomachean Ethics* X, 1177a 11.

of pleasure is ultimately the long, roundabout way of the justification of happiness as a higher pleasure: "It follows of strict necessity, Callicles, that the temperate man, as shown in our exposition, being just and brave and pious, is the perfection of a good man; and that the good man does well and fairly whatever he does; and that he who does well is blessed and happy, while the wicked man or evil-doer is wretched."[12]

Now, happiness, restored by the reflection on the "excellences" of the "good" man, is ultimately the highest form of the pleasant. The hierarchy of the good is a hierarchy of the pleasant itself which perfects the good. The pleasant is to the good what pleasure is to the accomplished vital function: an experienced perfecting felt as an analogue of pleasure. The pleasure discovered at the end of the ἐποχή of substantive pleasure is ultimately happiness as the acme of adjectival pleasure, the pleasant.[13]

That is what I understand prior to any reflection on evil or on the hostility of sensibility to law and on the coercion of duty. Moreover, I understand pleasure as "pathological," in the Kantian sense, only from the vantage of the primordial destination of pleasure, from its function of perfection with regard to the "good" on all the levels of human activity. And if it is true that I understand the affective amplitude of the pleasant via the detour of a reflection on the "virtues," I also understand these virtues prior to any downfall as a flowering or realization of man's potencies or functions. In short, I understand them as complete affirmation and not as coercion and negation. Duty is a function of evil; virtue is a modality or a differentiated form of the "destination" (*Bestimmung*) of the "function" (ἔργον) of man. Virtue is the affirmative essence of man prior to all downfall and all duty that forbids, constrains, and saddens.

At the end of this dialectic of the affective, where happiness served as a *critical theme* with regard to pleasure, it appears that the idea of happiness, worked out in the narrow framework of the dialectic of happiness and character, was only an idea, a demand for totality opposed to the individuality of an existential perspective. This idea has been enriched by an immense affective meaning. From now on

12. *Gorgias* 507c, in *Plato*, trans. W. Lamb, Loeb Classical Library (Cambridge: Harvard University Press, 1961), pp. 467–69 [Trans.].

13. *Nicomachean Ethics* X, 1177a 23.

it is the most excellent form of pleasure itself. In hierarchizing the various levels of pleasure, the idea of happiness receives from this very critique the affective plenitude that it lacked: it is the greatest of all pleasures.

This fullness of the life of feeling, which the Greeks realized in a meditation on happiness and pleasure, is rediscovered by contemporary psychology in different ways. On the one hand, the psychology of vital feelings has profited from all the studies on affective *regulations* having a functional character. On the other hand, the philosophy of spiritual feelings has profited from all the meditations on feelings that may be called ontological.[14] We must not sacrifice one for the other but rather use this dual invitation of contemporary thought as a means for renewing the ancient dialectic of pleasure and happiness.

Nowadays the "perfection" of the pleasure that "perfects" an action accomplished without impediment is called a regulative function. Every contemporary effort to distinguish the useful function of signaling, which is attached to the feeling of emotional disorder and all the other forms of disturbance, continue Aristotle's struggle against the moralizing and pathological depreciations of pleasure.

It is all the more striking since the rehabilitation of feeling as a regulator leads to the same difficulties as the Aristotelian justification of pleasure and its perfection in the instant. For feeling receives a functional justification only in a perspective of adaptation to the biological and cultural environment. Feeling points out how far along we are toward the resolution of tensions. Its modalities and its felt nuances mark the phases of action launched by a certain disequilibrium seeking a new equilibrium. Feeling is thus a function of the recovery of the person's equilibrium. To understand its role in this process is to understand feeling.

The difficulties begin with the recognition of the functional and regulative role of feeling. What is in question is the most general presupposition of this normativity, namely, the very idea of adaptation to a supposedly given environment. This doubt concerning the idea of adaptation rules all the other questions: what is the *validity* in human psychology of notions such as tension, resolution, equilibrium, readaptation? This question is not a repetition of the one we

---

14. Cf. the theory of cognitive emotion and feeling as found in the writings of Max Scheler, especially in *Wesen und Formen der Sympathie* [Trans.].

mentioned before in connection with the value of the metaphor itself. Here it is a question of the validity of transposing an adaptive schema that is valid in animal psychology into anthropology. This extension requires a critique whose principle is found in the Greek dialectic of pleasure and happiness.

Indeed, this extension is not illegitimate. Its heuristic and explanatory value would be incomprehensible if these concepts of adaptation did not describe a real human situation. But the situation that they accurately describe is characterized by *oblivion* and *dissimulation* of the ontological destination of human desire; it is a human situation reduced and simplified to the point of mimicking the vital in the cultural. Indeed, only vital functions of a periodic nature are, strictly speaking, subject to a criterion of adaptation because they have a finite resolution to their tensions. But in many ways we place ourselves in an analogous situation. Certain professional activities require the application of only an isolated part of our personality that we give, as it were, to a job. In an horizon limited by a precise task, adjustment can still be finite and measured according to norms of efficiency. Through this abstraction, in the strong sense of the word, man finds himself in a situation equivalent to that of vital functions with a finite ending. But this equivalence is provisional, because man *can* break through the boundaries of this abstraction: this is what happens when he puts his life above the performance of any finite task and looks upon his work as a means of earning a living. Then his desire outruns his work toward what he will be able to obtain through his work, which for him is no more than the social cost of his livelihood, leisure, and life.

To the extent that the social "roles" that we take on involve more indefinite tasks less susceptible of precise definition, the idea of adaptation lends itself *a fortiori* to less and less exact determinations and criteria. The fulfillment of a task can no longer be equivocally felt as a success. The feeling of being in one's place in society brings into play such complex things as a standard of living and particularly the way of life that a given craft imposes or permits. All the aspects of the personality are more or less implicated in this evaluation. Crafts or professions, in fact, present themselves as careers more or less "open" or "blocked" in which we can raise our level of pretention. Thus we ourselves are the origin of maladjustments that the social task does not univocally determine. The conditions of our adjustment are not only defined by the environment, but are also partially defined by the requirements evolved by our whole personality that expresses itself in the very level of our pretensions. Thus, in going from the idea of a task defined by norms to the idea of a level of pretension that is determined jointly by society and the subject's personality, we have introduced, in the very center of the ideas of equilibrium, adaptation, and adjustment, a factor of inexactness that tends to make them unusable.

But most often we treat ourselves as objects. Working and social life require this objectification; our very freedom depends on these social regularities which give us a routine existence. And so we create ourselves and in ourselves the conditions of validity of the concepts of modern psychology. These concepts are adapted to the man who adapts himself.

But this objectified existence—to say nothing of the "reification" which we shall speak of later—does not exhaust the fundamental possibilities of man. Taking the breadth of knowing as a guide once more, we may still uncover a corresponding breadth of feeling and challenge from the very outset the identification of feeling with affective regulation, toward which the psychology of adaptation tends.

If one could say that man's life, work, and even intelligence consist in solving problems, he would be wholly and radically definable in terms of adaptation. But more fundamentally man is a being who poses problems and raises questions—if only by bringing into question the very foundations of the society that bids him to adapt himself quietly to its system of work, property, law, leisure, and culture.

Every critique bearing on the very project of closed-system adjustment and finite adaptation feeds on this corrosive power of bringing into question.

It is here that motivational psychology, in demonstrating the inadequacy of its narrow confines, encounters philosophy and its dialectic of pleasure and happiness. For if the contemporary notion of affective regulation extends the ancient theory of pleasure, which, according to Aristotle, completes activity that is itself perfect, the meditation on the feelings that may be called spiritual and ontological extends the Platonic notion of "eros" that is but one aspect of Socratic "eudaimonism." Indeed, whatever the differences in the conception of Good and Being within the Socratic movement may be, all the Socratics attempt to sketch the portrait of the happy man.

But the psychology of feeling is blind without the philosophy of reason: that in affective confusion which distinguishes the happiness intention from the pleasure intention is reason, reason in the Kantian sense, reason as a demand for totality. Happiness has the same breadth as reason; we are capable of happiness because reason "demands the absolute totality of conditions for a given conditional thing."[15] In reason I "demand" what I "pursue" in action and that to which I "aspire" in feeling. Meaning, speech, the verb, which we questioned in the second chapter, and the practical reason, which already appeared to us in the third chapter in the empty idea of happiness, thus announced a corresponding moment of feeling that is like an affective openness in the closing of Care.

We may remember that excellent text where Kant—the philosopher who began by rejecting happiness as a principle of morality—rediscovers, at the root of every dialectic and every transcendental illusion, "a view [Aussicht] into a higher immutable order of things in which we already are, and in which we may, by definite precepts, continue our existence in accordance with the supreme decree of reason." This text makes it very clear what the reciprocal genesis of reason and feeling can signify.

On the one hand, reason, as an openness to the totality, engenders feeling as an openness to happiness. On the other hand, feeling interiorizes reason and shows me that reason is my reason, for through it I appropriate reason for myself. In Platonic language, we are of the race of ideas; the Eros that goes toward being is also that which recalls being as its Origin. In Kantian terms, reason is my "decree" and my "destination"—my Bestimmung—the intention according to which I can "continue my existence." In short, feeling reveals the identity of existence and reason: it personalizes reason.

No doubt we must say more about this subject if we wish to avoid falling back into a mere formalism that would allow the essence of the revelation of feeling to escape. In the above citation from Kant, it was a question of "this order in which we already are and in which we may continue our existence." Feeling is wholly itself only through

15. Critique of Practical Reason, "Dialectic of Pure Practical Reason" (Beck p. 212).

that consciousness of being already in . . . , through that primordial *inesse*. Feeling is more than the identity of existence and reason in the person; it is the very belonging of existence to the being whose thinking is reason.

Here we see in all its fullness, although in a confused anticipation, what we earlier called the identity of intention and affection in feeling, in which we recognized the counterpart of the duality of subject and object. Reason without feeling remains in the duality, in the distance. Whatever being may be, feeling attests that we are part of it: it is not the Entirely-Other but the medium or primordial space in which we continue to exist.

This fundamental feeling, this Eros through which we are in being, is particularized in a diversity of feelings of belonging that are, as it were, the schematization of it. These feelings, called "spiritual," are no longer adaptable to any finite satisfaction; they make up the pole of infinitude of our whole affective life. This schematization develops in two directions, that of interhuman participation in the various forms of "We," and that of participation in tasks of supra-personal works that are "Ideas." In the first direction the fundamental feeling schematizes itself in all the modalities of φιλία. The *inesse* takes the form of a *coesse*. The infinitude of feeling emerges clearly from the fact that no organized, historical community, no economy, no politic, no human culture can exhaust this demand for a totalization of persons, of a Kingdom in which, nevertheless, we now are and "in which, alone, we are capable of continuing our existence." This interhuman schema of being branches itself out into the form of receptivity to the most far-removed and the form of the affinity for what is close at hand. But I can no more separate the close from the far-removed than I can separate friendship for persons from a devotion to Ideas. The encompassing thing is this very dialectic of the forms of φιλία within the interpersonal relationship, to which correspond two views of one's fellow-man, *and* the greater dialectic of two modes of belonging—belonging to a "We" and belonging to "Ideas"—which manifest our inherence in being in its entirety. Interhuman participation is not possible without the consciousness of taking part in a creative theme that gives the general drift of its meaning to the community and thus endows it with a bond and a goal. It is always an Idea that gives a horizon of meanings to the growth of a "We" and a "friendship." This loving participation in ideas is the noetic or spiritual feeling *par excellence*. Nowhere else do we feel with such certainty that reason is not something alien but is rather a part of our very nature.

By means of this brief schematization of ontological feeling we come to what might be called the polarity of Heart and Care. The "heart" is at once the organ and the symbol of what we just called the "schemata" of ontological feeling. Here we find the interpersonal schemata of *being-with* as well as the supra-personal schemata of *being-for* and the fundamental intention of *being-in*. Here the Heart is always the polar opposite of Care; its fundamental openness or availability is always opposed to the greed of the body and living. Sacrifice is the dramatic form that, in a catastrophe, takes on the heart's transcendence; sacrifice attests that, at the limit of life, to give one's life for a friend and to die for an idea is the same thing. Sacrifice shows the fundamental unity of two schemata of belonging, the schema of friendship and the schema of devotion (or loyalty). Friendship is to another what devotion is to the idea, and the two together make up the view—the *Aussicht*—"into an order in which, alone, we can continue to exist."

This idea of a "schematization" of ontological feeling may enable us to solve a number of difficulties attached to the very notion of ontological feeling. First, if we take into consideration that feeling is here a promise more than an actual possession, the multiplicity of feelings with ontological intention or pretension is no longer a nullifying objection against the very idea of ontological feeling. Feeling anticipates more than it gives, and so all "spiritual" feelings are feelings of the transition toward happiness. Happiness, we said, is only designated by the "signs" of happiness, and these signs are accessible only from the point of view of a character. Accordingly, a typology of happiness has nothing contradictory in it, for there are many ways for an individual to feel oriented toward fulfillment: some linger in the signs and rejoice in them; another is more alive to the increase of his capacity for existence and experiences joy; another savors his victory in advance and he exults; another feels that his cup is full and abounds in thankfulness; still another feels relieved of the burden of existence, light, safe from all danger, and tastes a high degree of insouciance, an unalterable serenity, and peace of mind. Happiness would be all that at once and for always. What appeared to us elsewhere as a typology governed by the diversity of characters now appears to us as a schematization following the diversity of the initial situations out of which we apprehend this order in which we can continue to exist. One situation accentuates the interhuman bond and requires more attention to persons than to ideas; another situation accentuates the bond through the idea and makes feeling appear as a capacity of suffering for a Cause.

The same idea of the "schematization" of feeling may also allow us to account for feelings with an ontological bearing; this type of feeling, however, is not ruled by the belonging to "Ideas" or the belonging to a "We." These are feelings which are essentially form-less, moods,[16] *Stimmungen*, or, as someone has termed them, atmos-pheric feelings. We just enumerated some of them when we were speaking of the typology of happiness: delight, joy, exultation, se-renity. . . . Perhaps their profound significance appears in relation to the "schematized" feelings; they are, as it were, the counterpart of this schematization. Through their formless character they denote the fundamental feeling of which the determined feelings are the schemata, namely, man's very openness to being. To be sure, all at-mospheric feelings do not have this ontological intention: they are found at all levels of existence, particularly at the vital level (feel-ings of well-being, uneasiness, good or bad humor, lightness or heaviness, energy or fatigue, etc.). All feelings are capable of ac-quiring form or of returning to a formless state; this is a consequence of the intentional structure of feeling in general: in turn, it takes on form in accordance with the objects of knowledge to which it fastens its felt epithets, or returns to the formless in accordance with the law of interiorization, of introception, the plunging-back into the ground of life from which intentional acts emerge. This explains why the whole of the formless is not ontological; the formless is also hier-archized following the levels of activity that human existence tra-verses. However, if all atmospheric feelings are not ontological, it is understandable that the ontological does manifest itself through formless affective "moods." It might be said that the unconditioned, which is thought but not known by means of objective determina-tions, is experienced in a modality of feeling that is equally formless. If being is "beyond essence," if it is horizon, it is understandable that the feelings that most radically interiorize the supreme inten-

16. *Tonalités*, literally attunements, which we have translated by moods [Trans.].

tion of reason might themselves be beyond form. "Moods" alone can manifest the coincidence of the transcendent, in accordance with intellectual determinations, and the inward, in accordance with the order of existential movement. The height of the feeling of belonging to being ought to be the feeling in which what is most detached from our vital depth—what is absolute, in the strong sense of the word— becomes the heart of our heart. But then one cannot name it; one can merely call it the Unconditioned that is demanded by reason and whose inwardness is manifested by feeling.

Will it be objected, as a last resort, that ontological feeling does away with itself by dividing itself into negative and positive? Does not the clash of Anguish and Beatitude argue against the very idea of ontological feeling? Perhaps this clash has no other import than the distinction between the *via negativa* and the *via analogiae* in the speculation on being. If being is that which beings are not, anguish is the feeling *par excellence* of ontological difference. But Joy attests that we have a part of us linked to this very lack of being in beings. That is why the Spiritual Joy, the Intellectual Love, and the Beatitude, spoken of by Descartes, Malebranche, Spinoza, and Bergson, designate, under different names and in different philosophic contexts, the only affective "mood" worthy of being called *ontological*. Anguish is only its underside of absence and distance.

If man is capable of Joy, of Joy in and through anguish, that is the radical principle of all "disproportion" in the dimension of feeling and the source of man's *affective fragility*.

ΘΥΜΟ'Σ: HAVING, POWER, WORTH
(*avoir, pouvoir, valoir*)

The disproportion between the principle of pleasure and the principle of happiness points up the truly human significance of *conflict*. Indeed, feeling alone can reveal fragility as conflict. Its function of interiorizing, the inverse of that of the objectifying proper to knowing, shows that the same human duality that is projected in the synthesis of the object is reflected in *conflict*. We may remember that, for a merely transcendental analysis, the third term, the term of synthesis, the one Kant calls transcendental imagination, is nothing but the possibility of the synthesis in the object. It is in no way an experience capable of being dramatized; the consciousness to whose province it belongs is by no means self-consciousness, but the formal unity of the object, a project of the world. It is quite different with feeling. By interiorizing the duality that makes up our humanity, it dramatizes it in conflict. With feeling, the polemical duality of subjectivity replies to the solid synthesis of objectivity.

A study of the dynamics of affectivity, guided by the antinomy between the finite resolution of pleasure and the infinite resolution of happiness, can give stability and credence to what is still only a working hypothesis, a reading-guide. This study would extend the brief notations devoted to that θυμός in Book IV of the *Republic*. Plato, we remember, saw in this point the crux of human contradiction: sometimes it takes the side of desire in the form of aggressiveness, irritation, and anger; sometimes it enters the service of reason and becomes the power of indignation and the courage of enterprise. That is the direction we must pursue if we wish to elicit a third term that is no longer merely intentional and lost in the object, like the transcendental imagination, but accessible to the heart. For θυμός is properly the human heart, the heart's humanity.

We may place the whole median region of the affective life under the sway of this ambiguous and fragile θυμός, the whole region situated between the vital and spiritual affections, or, in other words, all the affectivity that makes up the transition between living and thinking, between βίος and λόγος. It should be noted that it is in this intermediate region that the *self* is constituted as different from natural beings and other selves. Living and thinking, whose specific affection we explored under ἐπιθυμία and ἔρως, are, respectively, shy of or beyond the *Self*. Only with θυμός does desire assume the characters of otherness and subjectivity that constitute a Self. Conversely, the Self overspills itself in feelings of belonging to a community or to an idea. In this sense the Self is a "between-two," a transition. Now, it is necessary to come upon this difference of the self from other selves prior to the self-preference that makes it hostile and wicked. Self-preference, which is fault or an aspect of fault, finds in this make-up of difference the structure that makes fallibility possible without making it inevitable. We must, then, dig or bore *underneath* the "passions" that, in man's historical and cultural life, mask the innocence of "difference" under the cloak of vain and deadly "preference."

This task is not easy. This problem was totally ignored by the

old *Treatises on the Passions*. Those treatises, of the Thomist or Cartesian type, deliberately stay within the dimension of desire with
finite termination and only occasionally encounter the opposition of
two affectivities, for example when they distinguish sense pleasure
and spiritual joy, or note their mutual hindrance, or the reverbera-
tion of the spiritual in the sensible. Because the affective dialectic
was not their principal object, they missed the problem of the intermediary, of θυμός.

St. Thomas' analysis of "the irascible" is revealing in this respect.
The irascible is not an original stage in the affective life, but merely
a complication and an added convolution of the concupiscible.
The concupiscible cycle begins with love (*amor*), culminates in
desire (*desiderium*), and closes with pleasure (*delectatio, gaudium,
laetitia*). In parallel fashion, hate (*odium*) ends in sorrow (*dolor,
tristitia*), passing through repulsion (*fuga*). These "passions" are
distinguished by their objects: the lovable, which is the good experienced as natural, appropriate, and suitable; the desirable, which
is the same good experienced as absent and distant; the pleasant,
which is the good possessed. It is the same *intention* of sensible
"good" and "evil" that modulates on satisfaction, lack, and presence,
and it is the specific "repose" of pleasure that gives direction to this
intentio (although the whole cycle takes its name from the more
sensible term, desire). This remark is important because all the passions are directed to this term, which is last in the order of execution, but first in the order of intention. The "irascible" does not really
break this cycle; it merely complicates it. In fact, it is to desire that
St. Thomas attaches these new passions that take their generic title
from one among them, anger; indeed, their object is only one aspect
of "good" or "evil": it is good or evil *qua* arduous, that is, difficult
to attain or difficult to overcome. It is this convolution of difficulty
which gives rise to the passions of opposition and combat: hope,
which holds the obstacle as proportioned to my forces and the good
as accessible; despair, which makes the good seem out of reach; fear,
which feels evil to be superior to my forces and invincible; boldness,
which feels equal to overcoming the obstacle; and lastly, anger,
which, when confronted by an already present evil, has no other resort than to rebel and retaliate against the aggressor. This discovery
of the irascible is certainly very valuable, but only within the limits
of a psychology of adaptation, of finite adjustment. Within these

limits it has the virtue of distinguishing the moment of aggressiveness as the long detour on the way to enjoyment of . . . , and it is regrettable that Descartes abolished this discovery by shutting up into one "passion," which he calls "desire," the Thomist desire, its contrary, repulsion, and the whole group of passions of the irascible: hope, despair, fear, audacity, and anger.

This Cartesian reduction of all the "irascible" to desire is not without foundation: it shows that the irascible does not really constitute an original affective level, but is a simple extension of the finite cycle (love–desire–pleasure; hate–repulsion–pain). Without fundamentally changing the sense of it, the difficult good, attainable or unattainable, and the difficult evil, invincible or vincible, remain sensible good and evil. Consequently, the passions of the irascible remain tributary to the valences of the concupiscible; the complication of *accessus* and *recessus* that they govern is only a lively episode in the march toward fulfillment, anticipated in the "satisfaction" of love and oriented by the *intentio quiescens* of pleasure.

And yet, careful description must contest this "intercalary" character of the irascible passions. On several occasions the postulate of this psychology, centered on goods to be used and consumed, falls short. The insertion of another person among the consumable objects toward which the sensible appetite is directed constitutes a turn that is singularly more decisive than the insertion of an obstacle and danger between desire and pleasure, or between repulsion and pain (inasmuch as the most important obstacles and dangers of life come from intersubjective reality). Now, satisfaction and union, on which the Thomist as well as the Cartesian treatise is patterned, is satisfaction with regard to and union with the good *qua* thing. We must even say that, strictly speaking, the description of the love–desire–pleasure cycle is valid only for the alimentary union; sexual love is not a desire for union in the same sense. The quests that traverse sexual love, which we shall come back to later, particularly the quest for reciprocity, bar it from being reduced, unless through immaturity or regression, to a need for orgasm whereby the other person would be only an accidental means and not an essential partner. Inherent in the very biological structure of the sexual need is the reference to external signals that immediately connect it to a counterpart of the same species who is irreducible to an object for consumption.

Love of friendship is *a fortiori* of a different order than concupiscent love. St. Thomas and Descartes, of course, were just as much aware of this as we are; and they detected the role of another person in many other passions besides love, e.g., in the fundamental passions of hate and anger, as well as in several other "derivative" passions—envy, jealousy, etc.[17] But they did not draw any theoretical conclusion from this. They continued to describe pleasure in general terms as that which perfects an unimpeded activity without distinguishing in this supererogatory perfection between, on the one hand, the mode of consummation peculiar to alimentary pleasure, and, on the other, the reciprocal union of friendship, and more generally the modes of "satisfaction" of other quests for which another person may be the correlate or the occasion. The "good" remains neutral, indifferent to the distinction between thing and person. The distinction between concupiscent love and love of friendship, between hate as repulsion and hate as a will to hurt, between anger as irrita-

17. Thus St. Thomas distinguishes love of friendship from concupiscent love. At first sight the difference is one only of accent; the first is directed toward *the one to whom* one wishes good; the second toward the *good* one wishes to another. The friend, however, is loved for himself, "but that which is another's good is only a relative good. Consequently, the love with which another is loved when one wishes him good is love pure and simple; and the love with which a thing is loved, that it may be another's good, is relative love" (*Summa Theologica*, I–II, q. 26, a. 4, corpus). In virtue of this, concupiscent love remains wholesome only as long as it remains subordinated to love of friendship, as the narcissistic component of love (cf. the remarks of a commentator on St. Thomas: M. Corvez, trans. *Somme théologique* [Desclée], I 218).

One could not better stress the upheaval introduced by *love for someone* in the description of love for *something*. It is all the more surprising since the theory of pleasure, with which the theory of love ends, no longer bears the trace of it. The example of anger is still more striking; it was first described as a rebellion against the evil already there; upon closer examination it reveals two objects: the revenge it desires, which is a good, and the adversary against which it revenges itself, which is an evil (q. 46). In virtue of this, the hate to which it is compared also appears as fundamentally intersubjective, insofar as it is willing someone evil. In this respect, its malice is even greater than that of anger, which, in seeking revenge, goes through a movement of retribution and therefore of punitive justice. The initial schema of hate is radically altered by this insight. In the framework of the psychology of the concupiscible, hate was merely an appetitive dissonance with respect to "that which is perceived as repugnant and harmful" (q. 29, art. 1, conclusion). This general definition does not allow one to foresee that the reference to others is essential to it.

tion against the obstacle and anger as revenge against another, was taken into consideration only momentarily, and in the end it was reduced to an accidental distinction within the idea of sensible "good" and "evil." Yet the encountering of another person is what breaks the finite, cyclic pattern of the sensible appetite.

The illustration of θυμός, therefore, must be looked for within the passions that are essentially (and not accidentally) interhuman, social, and cultural. In this respect, Kant's *Anthropology* goes further than the *Treatises on the Passions*. The trilogy of passions formed by possession (*Habsucht*), domination (*Herrschsucht*), and honor (*Ehrsucht*) is straightway a trilogy of *human* passions; from the outset it calls for typical situations of a cultural milieu and a human history; and likewise, from the very beginning it contests the validity of an indiscriminately human or animal schema of affectivity.

But with these passions of the Kantian *Anthropology*, the difficulty is the opposite of that of the Thomist and Cartesian *Treatises*. The latter could escape from moralism by reducing human affectivity to its animal root; the elementary passions were thus situated so as to favor the purificative and liberating enterprise of an Aristotelian psychology of pleasure. And so St. Thomas and Descartes could elaborate a "physics" and not an "ethics" of primary affections. By starting, on the contrary, with specifically human passions, Kant puts himself at once before the *fallen* forms of human affectivity. The *Sucht* of each of these passions expresses the modality of aberration or frenzy under which they enter into history. An anthropology elaborated from a "pragmatic point of view" is undoubtedly justified in proceeding in this way and in considering the "passions" as always already fallen. But a philosophical anthropology must be more demanding; it must attempt to restore the primordial state that is at the root of the fallen. Just as Aristotle described the perfection of pleasure beyond all "intemperance," so, too, must we discover an authentic *Suchen* behind this triple *Sucht*, the "quest" of humanity behind the passional "pursuit," the quest that is no longer mad and in bondage but constitutive of human praxis and the human Self. It is *necessary* to proceed in this way: for although we *know* these fundamental quests only *empirically* through their hideous and disfigured visages, in the form of greed and the passions of power and vanity, we *understand* these passions *in their essence* only as a per-

version of. . . . We must even say that what we understand at first
are the primordial modalities of human desire that are constitutive
with respect to man's humanity; and it is only later that we understand the "passions" as departure, deviation, downfall, in relation to
those primordial quests. No doubt the understanding of the primordial first, then of the fallen in and through the primordial, requires a kind of imagination, the imagination of innocence or a
"kingdom" wherein the quests for having, power, and worth would
not be what they in fact are. But this imagination is not a fanciful
dream; it is an "imaginative variation," to use a Husserlian term,
which manifests the essence by breaking the prestige of the fact. In
imagining another state of affairs or another kingdom, I perceive the
possible, and in the possible, the essential. The understanding of a
passion as bad requires the understanding of the primordial by the
imagination of another empirical modality, by exemplification in an
innocent kingdom.

Are we then bereft of any guide in this imagination of the essential? Not in the least. It is possible to understand what a non-passional
quest for having, power, and worth might be by referring these re-
spective affective steps to corresponding dimensions of objectivity.
If our theory of feeling is valid, the feelings that gravitate around
power, having, and worth ought to be correlative with a constitution
of objectivity on a level other than that of the merely perceived
thing. To be more precise, they ought to manifest our attachment to
things and to aspects of things that are no longer of a natural order
but of a cultural one. The theory of the object is by no means completed in a theory of representation; the thing is not merely what
others look upon. A reflection that would end the intersubjective
constitution of the thing at the level of the mutuality of seeing would
remain abstract. We must add the economic, political, and cultural
dimensions to objectivity; they make a human world out of the mere
nature they start with. The investigation of authentic human affectivity, therefore, must be guided by the progress of objectivity. If
feeling reveals my adherence to and my inherence in aspects of the
world that I no longer set over against myself as objects, it is necessary
to show the new aspects of objectivity that are interiorized in the
feelings of having, power, and worth.

The truly human quests establish new relations with other persons at the same time as a new relation to things. Strictly speaking, the mutuality of seeing is a very poor intersubjective relation. The "difference" of a Self from others is constituted only in connection with things that themselves belong to the economic, political, and cultural dimensions. Consequently, we must specify and articulate the relationship of the Self to another Self by means of the objectivity that is built on the themes of having, power, and worth.

This last remark also supplies us with a principle of order. We shall start with the quest for having, inherent in the passions of possession: here is where the relations to things govern most manifestly the relations to persons. In passing from the quest for having to the quest for power, we shall see the relation to others eclipse the relation to things to the extent that the sacrifice of having may turn into the austere way of domination. Finally, the quest for another's esteem makes a δόξα or quasi-immaterial "opinion" hold sway in the constitution of the self. But the relation to things, for all that, does not disappear: though less visible than in the case of having, the objectivity of the political and cultural level continues to orient the emergence of corresponding human feelings. This objectivity merely becomes more and more indistinguishable from the inter-human relation itself, the reality of which it consolidates into an institution.

Accordingly, we must first try to understand the passions of having—greed, avarice, envy, etc.—by reference to a possibly innocent quest for having. This quest is a quest of humanity in that the "I" constitutes itself therein by founding itself on a "mine." As true as it is that appropriation is the occasion for some of the greatest alienations in history, to that extent this second truth requires the first truth of an appropriation that is constituting before being alienating.

The object's new dimension that must now serve us as a guide is the economic dimension proper. Indeed, human psychology remains dependent on a theory of animal needs so long as it does not look for the principle of its specific nature in the object. A direct reflection on need cannot furnish the key to the economic sphere; on the contrary, it is the prior constitution of the economic object that can differentiate the truly human needs from animal needs. We do not know what man has need of before knowing what is economically a "good." The structure of human desire is too plastic and too undefined to provide political economy with a solid structure. It is precisely in becoming economic that this structure becomes human, that is, in relating itself to "available" things susceptible of being acquired, appropriated, and entering into the relation of the mine to the I.

This specific relation to the economic object carries a significance that neither the concupiscible nor even the irascible had when taken as animal tendencies linking the individual to a natural environment. The economic object is not merely a source of pleasure or an obstacle to be overcome; it is an *available* good.

This radical transformation of the animal "environment" into a human "world" is obviously related to the fundamental fact of work. The things to be desired and feared in a natural environment are not produced by the living being. Inasmuch as he produces his livelihood, man is a being who works. And because he works he establishes a new relation to things, the economic relation: whereas the animal merely preserves itself, man subsists and establishes himself among things in treating them as possessions.

We can bring out the originality of the "feelings" connected with having by moving back from the object *qua* economic object to the corresponding affectivity. Whereas the simple need is only an oriented lack, the desire for the economic object is relative to the object's *availability for me*. Insofar as the thing is "available" it creates the whole cycle of feelings relative to acquisition, appropriation, possession, and preservation. That which is properly feeling here is the interiorization of the relation to the economic thing, the reverberating of "having" in the I in the form of the "mine." The I, then, is affected by having, which adheres to me and to which I adhere. Through this feeling, I experience both my control over the having of which I can avail myself and my dependence with regard to that which is other than myself and on which I make myself dependent; I avail myself of it insofar as I am dependent on it; and I am dependent on it as a thing that can escape from me, degenerate, be lost, or be taken away: the possibility of no-longer-having is inherent in the tendency to avail oneself of. . . . The otherness of the mine, which is the breach between the I and the mine, is made up of the threat of losing what I have that is mine as long as I hold on to it. Possession is thus the ensemble of forces that hold out against loss.

In its turn this interiorization of the relation to the economic thing in specific feelings is contemporary with the specific modalities of the relation to another. Mine and yours, by mutually excluding each other, differentiate the I and the you through their spheres of belonging. Strictly speaking, the multiplicity of subjects is not a numerical multiplicity. Each *ego* retains a fringe of spiritual indifferentiation which makes communication possible and which makes the other my like. But the mutual exclusion, begun by the body insofar as it is a separate and occupied spatiality, is continued by mutual expropriation; the attachment to the body changes character through the interference of the attachment to the "mine." If I hold to my house because of my body, the relation to my body becomes, in turn, dependent on the economic relation to things that nourish it, clothe it, and protect it. Being established and settled completes incarnation and transforms it through and through. Moreover, the relation of appropriation invades the region of the mind step by step: I can be in a relation of appropriation with my thoughts (I have my ideas about that, I say). Straightway the mutual expropriation moves from the body to the mind and carries to completion even into their very inwardness the breach between the I and the you.

Does this mean that any innocence in having is unimaginable, that having is originally guilty and that human communion is possible only at the price of the deprivation of having? Certain historical forms of appropriation are no doubt incompatible with a total reconciliation. In this regard the nineteenth-century socialist critique has great significance. Nevertheless, I cannot *imagine* a suspension of having that would be so radical as to deprive the I of any anchorage in the "mine." If man's goodness is to be *possible*, even as a past or future utopia, this goodness would require the innocence of a certain having. It should be possible to draw a dividing line that cuts not between being and having, but between unjust having and a just possession that would distinguish among men without mutually excluding them. And even if all innocence had to be denied to private appropriation, the relation between man and having would still be reaffirmed on the level of a "We." Through the mediation of the "we" and the "our," the "I" would again join itself to a "mine." Thus, imaginative variation encounters a limit that bears witness to the resistance of an essence: I cannot imagine the I without the mine, or man without having. On the other hand, I can imagine an innocent relation of man to having in a utopia of personal and communal appropriation: the myth of paradise in which man possesses only what he cultivates, has only what he creates, a future utopia exemplifying the primordial relation of man to having, which in fact is always shown in history as an already fallen relation. I would never be able to educe the passions of having from this primordial relation, unless by means of some fantastic genesis. The forms of these passions springs endlessly from other historical forms. And psychology will never show me the birth of the impure. The imagination of an innocent appropriation has the function not of revealing an historical origin of evil but of constituting the "bad" significance of *Habsucht*, in grounding it upon the human quest for having and in designating *Habsucht* as a "perversion" of this primordial feeling.

The second root of self-affirmation, the one that perverts itself into *Herrschsucht*, is linked to a new situation of man, his existence within the relations of power.

This relation of man to power is irreducible to the preceding one even though it is partially implied in it. The power of man over man is even doubly implied in the relation of man to having, first in a technological sense, and secondly in an economic and social sense. We must keep in mind the essential difference between the two ways in which power is implied in having so as to understand the difference between the problems raised by political power and those raised by that derivative power implied in the relations of work and the relations of possession.

Work calls into play the power relations of man over man within the context of the relations of force between man and nature. Indeed, through work, human existence takes on the character of a rationally organized battle against nature that makes nature appear as a reservoir of forces to be conquered. It is through work that the difficult becomes a fundamental aspect of reality. Man's presence among things is a phenomenon of domination that makes man a force subjugating other forces. Now, the force of man's work also figures among the forces to be mastered. The rational organization of the battle against nature also implies an organization of human efforts in projects, plans, and programs. In this way man ranks among the number of resistances to be overcome by man. His work is a productive force to be organized: by means of his work he enters into relations of subordination. But this relation of subordination, inasmuch as it is a simple technological requirement, is merely one aspect of the rational organization of the battle against nature. While it is a subordination of operations and efficiencies, it is not yet a subordination of persons. Or, to be more precise, this subordination of operations becomes only in work itself a relation of command and obedience through the economic and social system and the institutional body that defines the form and no longer only the technology of work. The principle of the human hierarchization that work requires flows from the very task that is turned against natural forces. It is this task that works out a hierarchy of execution chiefly through the diverse connections between speech, which projects, plans, and imperatively prescribes the execution of the work, and the diverse modalities of the human gesture.

We see, then, that the relations of command, which are of a purely technological order, refer to relations of domination that spring from the socio-economic regime. It is quite evident that man's relations within the context of having introduce the power relations between men in work itself. The one who legally holds the means of production—the individual, group, or State—or even the one (individual or group) who simply controls them *de facto* or *de jure* as a manager, exercises power over the one who works. The capitalist conception of the entrepreneur who controls the work force because he owns the enterprise is only the most spectacular expression of this superimposition of economic domination and technological command. In other legal forms of the ownership of enterprise, this relation between the economic domination of work and the technological prescription of work changes its form, but it does not disappear: whoever is the property holder, there is always a man or a group of men who *utilize* the work force and for whom the work force is a means of production. In the most favorable case, the one in which the same group would economically utilize the work force and would carry out the work ordered by itself, the coincidence of the two functions of the social domination of work and the technological command in the same group of workers–owners would perhaps put an end to the alienated character of work. Yet it would not do away with the difference of the two relations of subordination, the technological one and the social one.

But in their turn, the relations of domination, which spring from the system of appropriating (private, collective, or State) the means of production, continue only because they are recognized and guaranteed by institutions sanctioned by an authority that is ultimately political. That is so true that the relations of socio-economic domination can be changed only by transforming the political structures of the power that puts the seal of institution on all the technological, economic, and social forms of man's power over man.

The political sphere is related to a theory of the passions through the phenomenon of power that is essential to it. And it is just as important to preserve power as to preserve having from a purely "passional" interpretation. Authority is not bad in itself. Control is a necessary "differentiation" between men and is implied in the essence of the political sphere. As Eric Weil says, "the State is the organization of an historical community. Organized as a State, the community is capable of making decisions."[18] Such a purely formal definition of the political sphere brings into play not only an organic body of institutions, but also the power of man over man. Whatever the origin of the State and its peculiar rationality—an indivisible and autarchic "nature" of the πόλις, according to Aristotle; a social contract, according to Hobbes and Rousseau; the objective spirit in history, according to Hegel—its power of organization and decision is exercised by one or a few men or, in the extreme case, all men. Sovereignty comes through the sovereign, the political sphere through politics, the State through power and government. Considered as power, the State has a monopoly on legitimate physical compulsion. In virtue of this it is the power of a few over all, a physical power to compel. In the lawful State this physical power of compelling coincides or would coincide with a moral power of exaction; but even in that case it would still be a power of man, an instituted power, to be sure, but an exercised power.

The objectification of man's power over man in an institution is the new "*object*" that can serve us as a guide in an immense world of feelings that manifest affectively the diverse modalities of human power according to which it is exercised, opposed, courted, or undergone. All the social roles that man may exercise initiate situations that political institutions consolidate into an object. Affectivity interiorizes these situations as intersubjective feelings that modulate indefinitely on the theme of commanding–obeying. It is quite obvious that no direct investigation of needs, tensions, and tendencies—even if they be called "psychogenic" in order to distinguish them from

18. Eric Weil, *Philosophie politique* (Paris: Vrin, 1956), p. 131.

"viscerogenic" needs[19]—can find its way in this affective maze. There is no end to constructing and ordering the varieties of feelings that revolve around the exercise of power, through all the modalities of influence, control, direction, organization, and compulsion. Psychological segmentation is endless; the ordering principle can come only from the "object," which here is nothing other than the form in which the interhuman relation of power is realized.

The feelings called "psychogenic" only interiorize the relation of the self to a new layer of objects that may, in a broad sense, be called cultural. Our theory of feeling, which is the correlative and the inverse of the process of objectification, finds here a new field of application: affectivity, that is to say, feeling itself inasmuch as it is experienced as a passive modification of the self, becomes human by making itself coincide with the objects of high order in which human relations crystallize. It is in the sense in which Hegel spoke of objective spirit that we speak of power and the institutions in which it takes form as an object. This political object, in return, is experienced according to the type of affective intentionality peculiar to feeling, in the feelings of power. The psychologist only discovers a formless constellation of "psychogenic" feelings, without being able to establish, in the absence of an objective guide and by direct inspection, their originality with regard to "viscerogenic" feelings.

On the other hand, these fundamental feelings are, for the psychologist, indistinguishable from the passions of power that Kant examines in his *Anthropology from a Pragmatic Point of View*. The essential distinction between the passional form and the feeling in which man's relation to power is constituted is not within the province of psychology. Here again it is a reflection on the object, on power considered as an established reality, which can bring out this essential distinction between the "destination for good" of power and its "disposition toward evil," as Kant puts it in his *Essay on Radical Evil*. It is on the object that I can imagine the "destination" of power, in the very core of its more or less perverse manifestations. To be sure, political power seems linked to evil—first of all because it counteracts the passions only by means of its corrective violence, as all the pessimistic philosophies of the individual, from Plato to Rousseau, Kant, and Hegel have noted; and secondly because, con-

19. Henry A. Murray, *Exploration in Personality* (New York: Oxford University Press, 1938).

sidered as a violent power, it is itself already fallen. The fact remains that I could not understand power as evil if I could not imagine an innocent destination of power by comparison to which it is fallen. I can conceive of an authority which would propose to educate the individual to freedom, which would be a power without violence; in short, I can imagine the difference between power and violence; the utopia of a Kingdom of God, a City of God, an empire of minds or a kingdom of ends, implies such an imagination of non-violent power. This imagination liberates the essence; and this essence governs all efforts to transform power into an education to freedom. Through this highly meaningful goal I "endow" history, in fact, with a meaning. By means of this imagination and this utopia I discover power as primordially inherent in the being man. In turning away from this meaning, in making himself foreign and alienated from this sense of non-violent power, man becomes alienated from himself.

Now, if this distinction between power and violence, imagined on the object, is carried over into the correlative affectivity of political objectivity, it is possible to imagine also the feelings that are at the root of the passions of power. These feelings are the source of the passions that derange them. These pure feelings, which are at work in the command–obey relationship, ground man as a political animal.

Behind the third passion in the Kantian anthropology, the passion of "honor," of glory, is a more primordial quest, the quest for worth in the eyes of another, the quest for esteem.

Nowhere is it more difficult to distinguish the perverse form from the constituting intention, the deranging passion from the constituting feeling: vanity and pretension seem to exhaust the whole illusory essence of this phantasmal existence of the I in another's opinion. Nowhere, however, it is more necessary to summon the alienated modalities of the I to its primordial essence. For it is at this point that the self is constituted: at the limits of the economic and the political spheres, and at the outer bounds of those feelings of belonging to a We, and of devotion to an Idea wherein we earlier distinguished a kind of affective schematization of philosophic Eros. In the quest for esteem there is a desire to exist, not through a vital affirmation of oneself, but through the favor of another's recognition. Between this quest for esteem, on the one hand, and the egoist and solipsist position on life, on the other, is all the distance that there is between mere desire and what the *Phenomenology of Spirit* calls the desire of desire.

The quest for reciprocity, which no will to live can account for, is the true passage from consciousness to self-consciousness. Now, this demand is not satisfied by the interhuman relations in the context of having, which are relations of mutual exclusion, nor by the relations in the context of power, which are asymmetrical, hierarchical relations, and therefore non-reciprocal ones. This is why the constitution of the *Self* is pursued beyond the economic and political spheres in the realm of interpersonal relations. It is there that I pursue the aim of being esteemed, approved, and recognized. My existence for myself is dependent on this constitution in another's opinion. My "Self," it may be said, is received from the opinion of others that establishes it. The constitution of subjects is thus a mutual constitution through opinion.

But the fragility of this existence as recognized is that the "esteem" that establishes it is merely "opinion," that $\tau\iota\mu\acute{\eta}$ is $\delta\acute{o}\xi a$. Here there is a threat of existing in a quasi-phantasmal manner, of being a reflection. The possibility of being no more than the word of another, the dependence on fragile opinion—these are precisely the occasion of the passions of glory that graft their vanity onto the fragility of esteem as opinion. This opining nature of esteem keeps the search for recognition within the median zone of affectivity, above the level of the will to live, and even above the feelings that cluster around having and power, but not within the sphere of Eros, which Plato said creates in beauty in accordance with the body and the soul: "The idea of creation [$\pi o\acute{\iota}\eta\sigma\iota\varsigma$]," says Diotima, "can be taken in many ways. For the cause of anything whatever that emerges from not-being into being is always an act of creation."[20] The mutual constitution of men in mutual esteem, as long as it remains opinion, is not yet within the sphere of that creation; and that is why it still pertains to $\theta\upsilon\mu\acute{o}\varsigma$ and not to $\check{\epsilon}\rho\omega\varsigma$. But Plato also says that $\theta\upsilon\mu\acute{o}\varsigma$ sometimes battles on the side of reason. Does not $\check{\epsilon}\rho\omega\varsigma$ find its best ally in this mutual esteem? Does it not embody itself in it when it *schematizes* itself in a common task that is both inhabited by an Idea and creative of a We in which individuals transcend themselves? Further-

20. *Symposium* 205b–c.

more, if θυμός can "battle on the side of reason," does this not take place when it overspills itself in an ardent quest for recognition by means of another esteem?

But if it is trying to situate this quest for esteem *between* the vital and the spiritual and *among* the "thymic" feelings that mediatize life and mind, it is still more trying to bring out its *own* constitution. Up to now we have made it our policy to let ourselves be guided by the constitution of objectivity for which feeling is the counterpart through interiorization. What is the objectivity here that follows up the objectivity of economic "goods" in the quest for having, and the objectivity of political institutions in the quest for power? It seems that there is no longer any objectivity at all.

It is nevertheless significant that this quest for esteem, dependent as it is on opinion, is named "recognition." For it is not enough to shore up the I with the mine, it is not enough to dominate in order to exist; I want to be recognized, too. Is it by chance that recognition derives from cognition? Only beings capable of cognition are beings capable of recognition. But on what constituted objects does recognition as feeling base itself?

It seems to me that we can say two things: Esteem involves a kind of objectivity, quite formal, it is true, which we can back up with a reflection of a Kantian style. The *quid* of esteem, *what* I esteem in others and for which I expect confirmation from others in myself, is what may be called our existence-worth, our existing worth. In this connection Kant says: "Rational beings are designated 'persons' because their nature indicates that they are ends in themselves," or "rational nature exists as an end in itself: man necessarily thinks of his own existence in this way."[21] Thus esteem indeed involves a representation, the representation of an end that is not merely an "end to be realized," but an "end existing by itself." The person as represented is just this. Now, this representation has a status of objectivity insofar as the worth of this end is not merely *for* us, but in *itself*. The opposition between the representation of an end in itself and that of a means for us is of itself constitutive of a dimension of objectivity. Not to be able to utilize another person is to encounter objectivity as a limit of my arbitrariness. Objectivity consists in that I cannot

21. *Foundations*, Beck pp. 86–87.

use another merely as a means, nor utilize persons like things: "Such beings are not merely subjective ends whose existence as a result of our action has a worth for us but are objective ends, i.e., beings whose existence in itself is an end. Such an end is one for which no other end can be substituted, to which these beings should serve merely as means. For without them, nothing of absolute worth could be found."[22] Kant gives the name of humanity to this objectivity. The proper object of esteem is the idea of man in my person and in the person of another.

I expect another person to convey the image of my humanity to me, to esteem me by making my humanity known to me. This fragile reflection of myself in another's opinion has the consistency of an object; it conceals the objectivity of an existing end that draws a limit to any pretension to make use of me. It is in and through this objectivity that I can be recognized.

It is necessary to add to this wholly "formal" objectivity of the *idea* of humanity the "material" objectivity of the cultural works that express this humanity? If the economic sphere is objectified in the goods and forms of having, and the political sphere in institutions and all the forms of power, then hyper-economic and hyper-political humanity is expressed in monuments that bear witness to this search for recognition. "Works" of art and literature, and, in general, works of the mind, insofar as they not merely mirror an environment and an epoch but search out man's possibilities, are the true "objects" that manifest the abstract universality of the idea of humanity through their concrete universality.

The promotion of objectivity, therefore, is pursued from having to power and from power to worth. The objectivity of having still adheres to that of things: through their "available" character economic goods are in the world like things. The objectivity of power is already that of a human relation made objective through institutions but connected to things through the physical power of compulsion that embodies the moral power of exaction. Cultural objectivity is the very relation of man to man represented in the idea of humanity; only cultural testimonies endow it with the density of things, in the form of monuments existing in the world: but these things are

22. Ibid., p. 87.

"works." It is this formal and material objectivity of the idea of man that engenders an affectivity to its measure: the cycle of the feelings of esteem.

What, then, is the moment of self-esteem? If our analysis of the corresponding objectivity is correct, my own self-esteem that I search for by means of the esteem of others is of the same nature as the esteem I experience for others. If humanity is what I esteem in another and in myself, I esteem myself as a thou for another. I esteem myself in the second person; in that case self-love, in its essential texture, is not distinct from sympathy, which means that reflective feelings do not differ from intentional feelings. I love myself as if what I loved were another; this otherness, which is linked to the feeling of valorization, makes up the difference between self-esteem and the attachment to life such as it wells up in catastrophic situations that threaten my life. Attachment to life or "vital" egoism is a short relation, direct from me to myself. Self-esteem or "thymic" egoism is an indirect relation, mediate from myself to myself in passing through the valorizing regard of another. Because the relation to self is an interiorized relation to another, opinion and belief are the core of it; worth is neither seen nor known but believed.[23] I believe that I am worth something in the eyes of another who approves my existence; in the extreme case, this other is myself. Insofar as I am affected by it, this belief, this credence, this trust, constitutes the very feeling of my worth. This appreciative affection, or this affective appreciation, is the highest point to which self-consciousness can be raised in θυμός.

This constitution of feeling starting from the object can serve as a guide in the labyrinth of the psychology of the feelings which gravitate around the worth of the self and which are glimpsed only through the more or less aberrant passional modalities. But an esteem experienced in a belief is what can err more than anything: because it is believed, the worth of the self may be sham, feigned, or alleged; it may also be neglected, contested, disputed, as well as scorned, belittled, choked back, and humiliated. And when, rightly or wrongly, it is neglected, the lack of esteem may be offset by a self-overestimation or by a depreciation of others and their values:

23. *Ni vue, ni sue, mais crue* [Trans.].

in this case aggressiveness, reprisals, resentment, and revenge are the defiant measures used against non-recognition, which itself can be understood only through the search for recognition. A filiation of affective significations may thus be attempted starting from the nucleus of beliefs that shore up the feeling of personal worth. When we try to understand others or ourselves we implicitly resort to this genesis of affective meaning: for it is not another or ourselves that we understand, but the content of belief, the noema of the feeling of worth in which the self and the other are constituted.

The possibility of a pathology of esteem is thus inherent in the very nature of esteem as opinion. Nothing is more fragile, nothing is easier to wound than an existence that is at the mercy of a belief; and one can understand how the "feeling of inferiority" could serve as a clue to the genesis of neuroses. Whatever the importance of this feeling in the etiology of neuroses, we must vigorously insist that the pathological forms of self-esteem are *understood* only in relation to its non-pathological and truly constitutive forms.

The same must be said about the specifically moral perversions of this feeling; its character of belief makes its corruptions possible: what is believed is presumed; and the presumption of the presumed can turn into the presumption of the presumptuous. The object of esteem, however, precedes the Nothing of glory. Between self-esteem and vainglory there is the whole distance that separates the possibility of evil and its advent: one has to be *blind* for vanity to pervert belief and for the quest for recognition to turn into a passion for honor. This blinding comes from elsewhere; it is not constituting but aberrant. Accordingly, it is not pathological self-love—in the Kantian sense of pathology—that explains feeling, but the primordial feeling that makes possible pathology in all the senses of this word.

AFFECTIVE FRAGILITY

The "disproportion" whose exegesis we have been pursuing through knowing, acting, and feeling takes on the name of fragility in the affective order. Fragility is the human duality of feeling, and we have looked for a first sign of this fragility in the differentiation of pleasure and happiness that *terminate* vital desire and intellectual desire. This first approximation of the idea of affective fragility suggests a way to continue our reflection. If ἐπιθυμία and ἔρως unfold

into two disparate manners of consummation, this disparity of pleasure and happiness must now be sought out in the mode of termination and completion of the "thymic" quests—having, power, worth.
Do these quests have a peculiar style of consummation? And how
does this style express the duality of pleasure and happiness?

It is the mode of fulfillment of θυμός, therefore, that reveals its unstable position between the vital and the "spiritual." Indeed, where
do the quests for possession, domination, and opinion terminate?

It is noteworthy that the Self is never certain: the triple quest in
which it seeks itself is never completed. Whereas pleasure is a kind
of provisory repose, as Aristotle so strongly established, and while
happiness would be *par excellence* a lasting peace, θυμός is restless.
To the extent that the "heart" is θυμός, the heart is essentially what
is restless in me. When will I have enough? When will my authority
be adequately grounded? When will I be sufficiently appreciated and
recognized? Where is the "sufficiency" in all that? Between the finitude of pleasure, which encloses a well-delimited act and seals it
with its repose, and the infinitude of happiness, θυμός slips a note of
indefiniteness and, along with it, the threat that clings to an endless pursuit.

All human action bears the mark of this indefiniteness. Θυμός upsets the structure of acts at the vital level, acts characterized by a
cycle of lack or avoidance, of pain, of initiating something, of attainment, of pleasure or pain. The criteria of "satiety" alone would
allow us to give a strict meaning to the idea of affective regulation;
but these criteria can no longer be applied. "Satiety" would be
reached if all the tensions could be totally saturated. But action,
insofar as it unfolds at the beck of the three fundamental quests of
self-being, is in principle a perpetual movement. The Thomist and
Cartesian description of the love–desire–pleasure cycle becomes unusable. Extending this cycle or introducing delays into it is no longer
sufficient; it is necessary to open it up. No action is any longer
terminal; all actions have become strangely intermediary.

Once again we see how insufficient is a complication of the cyclic
schema by the "arduous," the "difficult," or the "obstacle." For the
obstacle is still a vicissitude of actions with finite terminations. The
obstacle is linked up with one of the modalities of the means–end
relation, to the modality of "access"; and access, unlike the instru-

ment, which is also a modality of the means–end relation, presents the double valence of the desirable and the fearful. But this ambivalence is not sufficient to create a human situation radically different from the animal environment. The concept of a finite goal continues to characterize the relation of the obstacle to the intended end to which it bars access. Still more generally, the "technical" mediations elongate the itineraries of desire by interpolating preparatory media; but technical mediations ultimately refer to determined ends.

The originality of the desires of having, of power, and of worth lies in their undetermined terminus: the desire of desire has no end. A truly human situation is born as soon as a random desire is traversed by this desire of desire. At that moment results and success remain partial, relative to "tasks" that are projected on a background of non-saturated desirability; and this allows us to go onward. There even comes about this oddity: that the more exact our means become the more our ends become elusive in being overlaid with inter-human aims. This contrast between the technicity of means and the indetermination of ends contributes to that feeling of insecurity which invades actions without an assignable terminus. This residual desirability even changes the character of pleasure and pain, which turn from terminals into detonators for activity reactive to failure or to success. Thus, human action regenerates and nourishes itself of itself, drawn forward by its insatiable quests.

In this way human action takes on its character of *Streben*. For the human "conatus," pleasure and pain are no more than stopovers; and so the feelings of obstruction, hope and fear, timidity and audacity are drafted into the service of the specific feeling of indefinite action: courage, which is the second reaction to success and failure. Now, courage is another name for θυμός or the heart.

The fragility of feeling, which first appeared to us in the distention of pleasure and happiness, is thus summed up in the middle term, in the indefinitude of θυμός. But we must go further: θυμός is not merely "situated between" the vital and the spiritual; with regard to them it is the "mixture."

Affective fragility, then, will express itself in the exchanges between the indefinite quests of the self and the finite cyclic tensions on the vital level, and on the other hand between these same thymic quests and the desire for happiness. It is in these complex "endosmoses" that the "mediation" of θυμός is carried on.

Let us first consider the connections between the vital and the human: everything in us that may be called "instinct" (in an improper sense, because of the filiation from animal to man) is recast, transmuted, and brought to a level of humanity through the triple quest that makes us men. The case of sexuality is in this respect the most striking. Sexuality becomes human sexuality insofar as it is traversed, reconstituted, and penetrated by the truly human quest. That is why one can always detect in sexuality a note of possession, some nuance of domination, as well as a seeking for mutual recognition. It is even this last implication of human sexuality that introduces reciprocity into a relation which, by its biological roots, is fundamentally asymmetrical and which the desire of possession and of domination begin to humanize, but at the price of equality. All the richness of sexuality is here in this complex interplay of the vital and the human, itself so disparate. It follows from this that sexual satisfaction can no longer be simply a physical pleasure. The human being, through pleasure, beyond pleasure, and sometimes by sacrificing pleasure pursues the satisfaction of the quests with which "instinct" becomes overlaid; a certain indefiniteness thus enters into it while it is being humanized. Instinct becomes open and without end instead of cyclic. The whole Don Juan myth comes out of this.

Furthermore, this reconstitution and transformation of the vital into the human has as a counterpart a resurgence of θυμός within ἐπιθυμία. This is what Plato suggested by saying that θυμός fights on the side of desire. In my opinion the Freudian notion of libido could be reinterpreted in light of this idea borrowed from Plato. The libido is at once ἐπιθυμία and θυμός, desire and heart. When Freud says that the libido is sexual without being specifically genital, he very happily places his whole anthropological research within this unsettled region where coupling is also matching, where the desire for the opposite sex is desire for one's like. What Freud calls the "pleasure-principle" is already that mélange of the vital and the human, but with the vital predominant. The difference in sexual roles is essential to the libido, but through these roles there is the unlimited desire of affection that pursues its own dream. The fragility of these feelings remains in this twofold relation: genital desire is sublimated into tenderness beyond sex, whereas the desire for recognition, in embodying itself in tenderness, takes on a sexual coloring. This is why sexuality has an uncommon position in anthropology; it is the area of tenderness, at once deeply instinctive and profoundly human. It realizes in the extreme the desire of the other's desire, jointly ἐπιθυμία and θυμός.

But while θυμός undergoes the attraction of the vital, it also undergoes that of the spiritual. Thus a new "mixture" takes form in which it is legitimate to recognize the affective weft of great passions.

It is not by chance that we have passed such diverse and such incompatible judgments on the passions; there are many modes of passivity. Every feeling, insofar as the self is *affected* by it, is a passion.[24] It was out of consideration for this passivity of affection that the old treatises on the passions included under their title the whole field that we here call feeling; we are not taking passion in this sense. We reserve the name passion for a class of feelings that cannot be accounted for by a simple derivation from the vital feelings, by a crystallization of emotion, or, in general, in any way in the horizon of pleasure. Rather, we are thinking of those great ventures that constitute the dramaturgy of human existence, of Othello's jealousy, of Rastignac's ambition. It is all too clear that these are by no means complications of those fundamental "passions" that tradition has named love, hate, desire, hope, fear, boldness, timidity. A transcending intention dwells in them, and this can flow only from the infinite attraction of happiness. Only an object capable of adumbrating the whole of happiness can summon so much energy, lift man above his ordinary capacities, and make him capable of sacrificing his pleasure while living painfully. However, neither does one account for great passions, I mean the grandeur of passion, by hastily resorting to a principle of "unreason," of "illusion," to a vanity that would be the immediate expression of a principle of evil. A principle of pleasure added to a principle of illusion does not make up passion: "Nothing great," says Hegel, "has been accomplished nor could ever be accomplished without passion. A morality which condemns passion simply because it is passion is a deadly and too often a hypocritical morality."[25] The inordinate implies grandeur; the enslave-

24. *Pâtir*: literally, a suffering in the sense of being passive and acted upon [Trans.].

25. *Philosophy of the Spirit*, in *Encyclopaedia of the Philosophical Sciences*, remark on paragraph 374.

ment of the passions is the fallen modality of the impassioned life. The "passion"[26] of fascination, of captivity, and of pain would be incomprehensible if passional alienation were not coeval with a primordial grandeur, with an *élan*, with a transcending movement in function of which "idols" of happiness are possible. Neither passion-affection nor passion-unreason accounts for this transcending movement of the "great" passions. It is necessary, therefore, to connect passion to the desire for happiness and not to the desire to live. Indeed, man puts all his strength and his whole heart into passion because a subject of desire has become all for him. This "all" is the mark of the desire for happiness: life does not want all; the word "all" has no meaning for life, but only for the mind: the mind wills the "all" and thinks the "all" and will be at peace only in the "all."

But neither is passion a vague expectation of happiness, a demand in the Kantian sense. I see in passion the "mixture" of the unlimited desire, which we called θυμός, and the desire for happiness. If the impassioned person wants "all," he puts his "all" into one of those objects that we have seen become constituted in correlation with the I of possession, of domination and valorization. That is why I would readily speak of the schematization of happiness in the *élan* and in the objects of θυμός. One of those objects suddenly represents, in a kind of affective immediacy, the all of the desirable. One might say that the infinitude of happiness descends into the indefiniteness of restlessness. The desire of desire, soul of θυμός, proffers its objects in images and in ostensive representations to the objectless aim of happiness. Here is the source and the occasion of every mistake and all illusion. But this mistake, this illusion, presupposes something more primordial that I call the affective figuration of happiness in θυμός.

It is from this affective figuration of happiness in θυμός that passion draws all its organizing force, all its dynamizing action. For passion receives from Eros all its power of devotion, of *abandon*; all its *restlessness* from θυμός. That abandon and that undefined restlessness are anterior to the false infinite of passional madness and wed to a degree of profundity which this madness presupposes. The moment of abandon is familiar to us: it comes out of the participation in an Idea, in a We, wherein we recognized the essence of spiritual

26. *Pâtir* [Trans.].

desire. A passional life is a devoted life, dedicated to its theme: this "passivity" is more primordial than passional captivity and sufferance; all the other passive modalities of passion are grafted onto this first "passion."[27] On the other hand, this abandon, wherein we recognized the genius of Eros, is connected to the restlessness peculiar to the themes of θυμός: the impassioned man puts his whole capacity for happiness on the "objects" in which a Self is constituted. This shifting of the totality onto the "objects" of the cycle of having, power, and worth constitutes what we call the schematization of happiness in the themes of θυμός.

This schematization, which in a way extends that of the transcendental imagination into feeling, is the primordial fact that any passional transport presupposes. Only a being who wants the all and who schematizes it in the objects of human desire is able to make a mistake, that is, take his object for the *absolute, forget* the symbolic character of the bond between happiness and an object of desire: forgetting this makes the symbol an idol; the impassioned life becomes a passional existence. This forgetting, this birth of the idol, of servitude and passional sufferance, falls within the domain of a hermaneutics of the passions that we will undertake elsewhere. It was necessary, however, to show the point of impact of the passions in a primordial affection that is the very locus of fallibility. The restless devotedness of the impassioned is as the primordial innocence of the passional, and at the same time the essential fragility whence it originated. Nowhere better than in the relation of the impassioned to the passional do we understand that the structures of fallibility make up the pre-existing ground of fault.

The universal function of feeling is to bind together. It connects what knowledge divides; it binds me to things, to beings, to being. Whereas the whole movement of objectification tends to set a world over against me, feeling unites the intentionality, which throws me out of myself, to the affection through which I feel myself existing. Consequently, it is always shy of or beyond the duality of subject and object.

But by interiorizing all the connections of the self to the world, feeling gives rise to a new cleavage, of the self from the self. It makes perceptible the duality of reason and sensibility that found a resting-

27. *Pâtir* [Trans.].

place in the object. It stretches the self between two fundamental affective projects, that of the organic life that reaches its term in the instantaneous perfection of pleasure, and that of the spiritual life that aspires to totality, to the perfection of happiness.

This disproportion of feeling gives rise to a new mediation, that of θυμός, of the heart. In the order of feeling this mediation corresponds to the silent mediation of the transcendental imagination in the order of knowledge. But whereas the transcendental imagination is entirely reduced to the intentional synthesis, to the project of the object before us, this mediation is reflected in itself in an indefinite affective quest wherein is evinced the fragility of the human being. It seems, then, that *conflict* is a function of man's most primordial constitution; the object is synthesis; the self is conflict. The human duality outruns itself intentionally in the synthesis of the object and interiorizes itself affectively in the conflict of subjectivity. Even if it is true that the real conflicts that stake out affective history are accidents, in the literal sense of the word, random encounters between our effort, our power of affirmation, and the forces of nature, or the familial, social, and cultural environment, the fact remains that all these external conflicts could not be interiorized if a latent conflict within ourselves did not precede them, did not gather them in and bestow upon them the note of inwardness that it has from the outset. No conflict between ourselves and some process susceptible of conferring upon us an assumed personality could be introjected if we were not already this disproportion of βίος and λόγος, of living and thinking, of which our "heart" suffers the primordial discord.

CONCLUSION

The Concept of Fallibility

WHAT IS MEANT by calling man fallible? Essentially this: that the *possibility* of moral evil is inherent in man's constitution. This reply calls for two kinds of clarifications. It may be asked, indeed, in what features of this primordial constitution the possibility of failing resides more particularly. On the other hand, one may ask about the nature of this possibility itself. Let us consider these two aspects of the problem in succession.

LIMITATION AND FALLIBILITY

A long philosophic tradition, which attained its most perfect expression in Leibniz, would maintain that the limitation proper to creatures is the occasion of moral evil. Considered as the occasion of moral evil, this limitation would even merit the name of metaphysical evil. Our whole preceding analysis tends to rectify this ancient proposition in a precise way: the idea of limitation as such cannot bring us to the threshold of moral evil. Not just any limitation constitutes the possibility of failing, but *that* specific limitation which consists, for human reality, in not coinciding with itself. Nor would it be of any use to define limitation as a participation in nothingness or not-being: we remember that Descartes, *before* elucidating the relation of the will to the understanding, elaborated a brief ontology of human reality that consisted in combining the idea of being or perfection with "a certain negative idea of nothingness, i.e., of what is infinitely far removed from every kind of perfection." Thus he could say "I am a something intermediate between God and nothingness." But any combination of being and nothingness does not constitute the occasion of failing, for every reality that is not being as such is, in a quite general sense, "intermediate between God and nothingness." We can understand how Descartes could be satisfied with that brief outline: he intended not to set forth an ontology of human reality but merely to brush aside the hypothesis that man is endowed with a positive power of erring that would argue against divine perfection. In showing that man is composed of being and nothingness, he left room only for the idea of a default in being and ascribed the privative factor that is conjoined to this simple default to the bad use of the will. And so a brief ontology of the creature in general was enough to acquit God, and a philosophy of the faculties enough to indict man. Descartes' purpose here is purely apologetic; he makes no claim whatsover of determining the mode or the degree of being peculiar to man. But if we undertake to formulate such an ontology, the idea of limitation as such can no longer account for the idea of fallibility: what we need is a concept of human limitation that is not a particular instance of the limitation of the something-in-general. As Kant showed with respect to the categories of quality, there is nothing more in the idea of limitation than the synthesis of the positing and negating of something. Now we have need of a concept of limitation that is straightway one of human limitation.

The idea of "disproportion" seemed to us to satisfy this demand for a direct ontology of human reality that unfolds its particular categories against the background of a formal ontology of the something-in-general. The general concept of limitation belongs to such a formal ontology; but we cannot pass from the *specification* of the limitation of something to man's limitation. We must put in the particular categories of human reality.

These categories peculiar to human limitation must be disengaged directly from the disproportionate relation of finitude to infinitude. It is this relation that constitutes the ontological "locus" which is "between" being and nothingness, or, in other words, man's "degree of being," his "quantity of being." *It is this relation that makes human limitation synonymous with fallibility.*

Let us try to disengage those specific categories of human limitation by initiating a kind of "transcendental deduction," that is, a justification of concepts through their power of making a certain domain of objectivity possible. If we could show that these categories are the condition of possibility of a certain discourse on man, these categories would receive all the legitimation that one could require.

Accordingly, we shall complete our enterprise of total reflection on the *pathétique* of misery by elucidating those conditions of possibility of a discourse on man. Moreover, the myth of mélange and the rhetoric of misery include an implicit understanding, in the mode of "right opinion," of these categories themselves. The concepts of "mélange" and "intermediacy," characteristics of the great rhetoric on the human condition, are already existential categories, but adumbrated in the pathetic mode. That reflection can recapture them as categories, Plato himself assures us when he passes from the myth of "mélange" to the idea of μεταξύ and "mixture." The etymological continuity from the rhetorical theme of "mélange" to the dialectical notion of "mixture" assures us that the grace of language is with us in this enterprise.

Our guide in this deduction of the categories of fallibility will be the Kantian triad of the categories of quality: reality, negation, limitation. Why privilege this triad at the expense of that of quantity, relation, and modality? Because nowhere else does the transcendental deduction so clearly go beyond a strictly epistemological reflection bearing on the *a priori* constitution of the physical object to bring itself nearer to a transcendental phenomenology centered on the manifestation or the appearance of the object in general. What Kant says of the schemata of quality suggests of itself the free use we propose to make of the corresponding categories: "Reality," he says, "in the pure concept of understanding, is that which corresponds to a sensation in general; it is that, therefore, the concept of which in itself points to being [*ein Sein*] (in time). Negation is that the concept of which represents not-being [*ein Nichtsein*] (in time). The opposition of these two thus rests upon the distinction of one and the same time as filled and empty." In this way, there arises the schema of degree or a quantum of reality that is nothing other than the "quantity of something insofar as it fills time."[1] Disregarding Kantian orthodoxy, we shall not seek to transcribe this triad into a *science* of the degrees of sensation.[2] Rather, we shall transpose it onto the level of a philosophical anthropology so as to systematize the language employed throughout the course of this book.

In passing from an axiomatics of physics to a philosophical anthropology, the triad of reality, negation, and limitation may be expressed in the following three terms: *originating affirmation, existential difference, human mediation.* Our study expresses the pro-

1. *Critique of Pure Reason*, A143 (Kemp Smith p. 184).
2. J. Vuillemin, *Physique et métaphysique kantiennes* (Paris, 1955).

gression of this triad through knowing, acting, and feeling. What is in play in this dialectic is a more and more concrete determination of the third term that truly represents man's humanity.

Rather than recapitulating this concrete dialectic such as we have set it forth, we shall elucidate its founding concepts so as to show how they *make possible* an anthropology worthy of being called philosophical.[3]

First, it turns out that the initial guiding concept of such an anthropology is not and cannot be that of finitude. In this dialectic finitude is the result and not the origin. In this sense we must admit that Kant is right when he first posits the idea of a rational being in general, then restricts this idea by the difference of a sensibility to bring forth that of a *finite rational* being. This explains why the first crest in our own analysis is the one that passes through the three moments of originating affirmation, namely the Verb, the practical totality or the idea of happiness, and Eros or the happiness of the heart. From the first of these moments to the second, from the second to the third, originating affirmation becomes progressively richer and more inward: at first it is only the vehemence of the Yes, which has for a correlate the "is" that is signified—or, to be more precise, suprasignified—by the Verb. This is the "transcendental" moment of originating affirmation. This moment is necessary but not sufficient; it is necessary to make the power of existing pass from the register of "living" to that of "thinking"; it is insufficient to assure us that *we are* that thinking. It is ourselves that we affirm next in the practical idea of a totality which we approach through the understanding, always in process but never completed, of all the projects of all men and against which the enclosure of our character stands out. This essential openness or accessibility to ἔργον, to the "function" or the "project" of man as such, grounds the person in giving him a horizon of humanity that is neither I nor you but the task of treating the person, in me and in you, as an end and not as a means. The person is not decipherable directly without the guide of the idea of humanity that gives the person a goal. In this sense, humanity, understood as a totality to-be-made-to-be, is the condition of possibility of the person. But if the idea of humanity is capable of leading from the transcendental to the practical, it does not yet tell us that we *are*

3. With regard to this, cf. "Négativité et affirmation originaire," in *Aspects de la dialectique* (Paris: Desclée De Brouwer, 1956), pp. 101–24.

this humanity of thinking. It is Eros, it is Love that shows that this aim, which is immanent to the function of man, is happiness anticipated in a consciousness of direction and of belonging. Feeling alone, through its pole of infinitude, assures me that I can *"continue my existence in"* the openness of thinking and of acting; the originating affirmation is felt here as the Joy of "existing in" the very thing that allows me to think and to act; then reason is no longer an other: I am it, you are it, because we are what it is.

But the originating affirmation *becomes* man only by going through the existential *negation* that we called perspective, character, and vital feeling. Before Descartes and ever since the Platonic myth of Poros and Penia, we have known that man is intelligible only through participation "in a certain negative idea of nothingness." From Hegel to Sartre we have been told that man is this very negation. But what has been lost in the course of this victorious march of negation is its true relation to the power of affirmation that constitutes us. The problem of the "for-itself" of *man* is by no means resolved in its opposition to the "in-itself" of *things*. Such an opposition of a nihilizing "for-itself" and a reified "in-itself" still leaves the two terms external to each other and leads less to a dialectic than to a dichotomy between a stable "being" and a "nothingness" that uproots and isolates itself. The description of "nihilizing acts"—from absence to refusal, to doubt, and to anguish—certainly accounts for the promotion of man as non-thing; but the thing's being that man nihilizes is not the whole of being. And even when the "in-itself" represents my own dead past, my evolved being, the "having-been" (*gewesen*) of my existence, hardened into essence (*Wesen*), it is still external being that I rise up against. If contemporary philosophy has overvalued the nothingness of rupture and isolation to such a degree, it is through a disavowal of the originating affirmation or, as Spinoza says, of the effort to exist, identical to actual essence, which is wholly power to *posit* (*ponere*) and not to *do away with* (*tolere*). This is the being in question in man's being. Being is here affirmation, yes, joy. I do not thrust this being aside as the already transpired and dead; I am it and I participate in it.

Existential negation is a negation of this affirmation. No negation is more inward to being than this one. It is no longer a question of a nihilizing retreat from the having-been, but from the manifestation of the Verb in a perspective that denies it, of the totality of ends in a character that denies it, of love in an attachment to living that denies it. If we follow the course of this existential negation from the exterior toward the interior, it first appears as a difference between me and the other, then as a differing of myself from myself, and finally interiorizes itself in the sadness of the finite.

The most elementary reflection on perspective contains this whole process of thought in epitome; for I know perspective as perspective only as transgressed by the truth-intention; but I verify this transgression only through the opposition of perspectives other than mine. Thus when we speak of "several" consciousnesses, this is not to be taken as a simple arithmetical plurality; the otherness of consciousnesses is relative to a primordial identity and unity that makes possible the understanding of language, the communication of culture, and the communion of persons. Thereby another is not only an other, but my like. Conversely, this fundamental unity of λόγος is relative to the difference of λέγειν.[4] This difference signifies that the unity of humanity is realized nowhere else than in the movement of communication. Thus, difference is not absolute, as if the multiplicity of consciousnesses were purely numerical and their coexistence merely contingent, nor is the unity of the being man absolute, as if the impure causality of bad will alone would generate the splintering of consciousnesses. Man is this plural and collective unity in which the unity of destination and the difference of destinies are to be understood through each other.

By becoming interiorized, the difference between myself and the other becomes a difference of myself from myself; it is a difference no longer between destines but, in the center of an individual destiny, between its need and its own contingency. The need, in Kantian terms, is the totality that reason "demands" (*verlangen*); in Aristotelian terms, it is the happiness man "pursues" (ἐφίεσθαι) in his action. The contingency of character is what expresses this need. This consciousness of contingency is more inward to the primordial affirmation than was the consciousness of my difference from others; the latter still rested on the feeling that the quantity of reality that I am excludes the immense possibilities of humanity realized by others and *not* by myself. The feeling of difference left the otherness out-

4. λόγος, the faculty of reason; λέγειν, the verb to talk, which can mean speaking, exhibiting, recounting, setting forth, etc. [Trans.].

side of me, but the feeling of contingency interiorizes it; in it the need reverses into its contrary. That which I *am to be* is denied in the feeling that it was not necessary that I be such as I am, nor even that I exist, that it was possible for me to have been another and even not to have been. This feeling cannot be stated without absurdity since the imagination of my being-other stands out against the background of the unquestionable presence of this body and of this life that excludes *ipso facto* all other possibilities; but the brute fact of existing in such a way, here and now, when it is measured against the demand for totality, emerges as existence that I do not produce, that I do not posit. Existence is discovered to be *only* existence, *default of being-through-self*. The imagination that forms the possibility there was of not being is, as it were, the revealer of that default of being-through-self. I did not choose to exist, existence is a given situation: that is what language brings out in the rational sign of non-necessity or contingency. I am here, and it was not necessary; a contingent being who reflects on his existence in the categories of modality must think of it as non-necessary; and this non-necessity exhibits the negativity shrouded in all the feelings of precariousness, of dependence, of default of subsistence, of existential dizziness, which come of the meditation on birth and death. In this way there arises a kind of coalescence between this lived dizziness and the language of modality: I am the living non-necessity of existing.

It is this non-necessity of existing that I live in the affective mode of sadness. "By sadness," says Spinoza in the *Ethics*, "I mean a passion by which the soul moves to a lesser perfection." Besides the sadness that expresses the intermittent character of my effort to exist, there is a ground of sadness that may be called the sadness of the finite. This sadness is nourished by all the primitive experiences that, to express themselves, have recourse to negation: lack, loss, dread, regret, deception, dispersion, and irrevocability of duration. Negation is so obviously mixed in with them that we can indeed hold this experience of finitude for one of the roots of negation.[5] It must be

5. I do not say that the negation of finitude is the sole root of negation. No doubt one must give up the idea of unifying the origin of negation. The idea of otherness, such as Plato first elaborated it, is linked to the operation of "distinguishing" that belongs to objectifying thought: the constitution of the perceived thing, of living individuality, of the individual psyche, presupposes the distinction of the something and another thing. The objective distinc-

admitted as a primary fact that some feelings have a certain affinity for negation in language because they are negatives. Negative language, such as it is formed in the objective sphere, principally through the operation of discrimination or distinction that separates the same from the other, offers itself for the expression of these lived moods. Need is expressed in an "I do not have," regret in a "no longer," impatient desire in a "not yet." But spoken negation would not suit these affects if it did not manifest a negative lying deeper than all language and which we may epitomize, following Spinoza, in the excellent word "sadness." This lessening of existence affects the very effort through which the soul endeavors to persevere in its being, and so it may well be called a primitive affection. Sufferance in all its forms exalts this negative moment implied in many affects; in suffering, consciousness isolates itself, retires into itself, and feels denied.

If such is the dialectic of originating affirmation and existential difference, it becomes understandable that "limitation"—Kant's third category of quality—is immediately synonymous with human fragility. *This* limitation is man himself. I do not think man directly, but I think him through composition, as the "mixture" of originating affirmation and existential negation. Man is the Joy of Yes in the sadness of the finite.

This "mixture" has appeared to us as the progressive manifestation of the *fault*[6] that makes of man, mediator of the reality outside of himself, a fragile mediation for himself.

The synthesis of the object is the silent synthesis of Saying and of Appearing, but *in* the thing itself, on the object. If this synthesis can be called consciousness, it is not self-consciousness. The transcendental imagination that makes it possible remains an art concealed in the depths of nature. The synthesis of the person endows the mixture with a practical sense and no longer a theoretical one; but this mixture remains a task. Mediation is sought through the varieties of the "mean" ($\mu\epsilon\sigma\acute{o}\tau\eta\varsigma$) which Aristotle worked out in the *Nicomachean Ethics* and which was not so much the golden mean of virtue as the difficult path of practical conciliation that threads its

---

tion is just as primitive a root of negation as the negative affects that make up the sadness of the finite. We shall come back to this in the third volume of this work.

6. Fault (*faille*) in the geological sense [Trans.].

way between the opposed abysses, represented by the diverse, disconnected forms of acting. Man even projects these "means" outside of himself. He projects them in works—the works of the artisan, of the artist, of the legislator, of the educator. These monuments and institutions extend the synthesis of the thing. The thing was *understood* in the unity of Saying and Seeing; the work is *made* in the unity of Sense and Matter, of Worth and Work. Man, artisan, artist, legislator, educator, is for himself incarnated because the Idea is in itself materialized. In particular, the work of art *endures* because the Idea it incarnates is saved from oblivion by the *durable* elements of the cosmos. But the discipline of the finite, dear to Goethe, effects the synthesis of need and contingency only in a new correlate of man, and this is precisely the "task." In himself and for himself man remains torn.[7]

It is this secret rift, this non-coincidence of self to self that feeling reveals. Feeling is *conflict* and reveals man as primordial conflict. It shows that mediation or limitation is only intentional, aimed at in a thing or in a task, and that for himself man suffers disunion. But this discord that man lives and suffers approaches the truth of language only at the end of a concrete dialectic that discloses the fragile synthesis of man as the *becoming of an opposition*: the opposition of originating affirmation and of existential difference.

FALLIBILITY AND THE POSSIBILITY OF FAULT

If the capacity to fail consists in the fragility of the mediation that man effects in the object, in his idea of humanity, and in his own heart, the question arises concerning the sense in which this fragility is a capacity to fail. What capacity is this?

Weakness makes evil possible in several senses that may be classified in an increasing order of complexity from the *occasion* to the *origin* and from the origin to the *capacity*.

In a first sense, it may be said that man's specific limitation makes evil merely possible; in this case fallibility designates the *occasion*, the point of least resistance through which evil can enter into man; the fragile mediation appears then as the mere space of the appearance of evil. Man, center of reality, man, reconciler of the extreme poles of the real, man, microcosm, is also the weak link of the real.

7. *Déchirement* [Trans.].

But between this possibility and the reality of evil, there is a gap, a leap: it is the whole riddle of fault. In the language of Scholasticism, which was still common to Descartes, there is no unbroken path from "default" to "privation." In the terms of Kant's *Essay to Introduce into Philosophy the Concept of Negative Grandeur*, evil is "a nothing of privation" that implies real opposition, actual repugnance, something the idea of fragility could not account for.

This gap between the possibility and the reality is reflected in a similar gap between the mere anthropological description of fallibility and an ethic. The first is prior to evil, the second finds the real opposition of good and evil. The most fundamental presupposition of every ethic is indeed that there is already a cleavage between the valid and the non-valid and that man is already capable of the dual: of the true and the false, of good and evil, of the beautiful and the ugly. Objectivity itself, which in the transcendental perspective was merely the unity of sense and presence, becomes, in an ethical perspective, a goal that may or may *not* be attained. Objectivity, which is synthesis *par excellence*, splits, as truth-value, between the valid and the non-valid. The same holds true for action. We have seen that man is by destination a mediation between the demand for happiness and the contingency of character and of death. But for ethics this mediation is a task, the task of working out a "mean," as Aristotle says, between the bad extremes. Taste itself, in the aesthetic realm, likewise implies a bad taste as opposed to it, although the idea of taste *can* be constituted, as in the *Critique of Judgment*, without reference to this contrary through the mere consideration of the free play of representations and of "pleasure without concept." Thus, ethics, taken in the broadest sense of the word, which takes in the whole realm of normativity, always presupposes man as having already missed the synthesis of the object, the synthesis of humanity in itself, and its own synthesis of finitude and infinitude; that is why ethics would fain "educate him" by means of a scientific methodology, a moral pedagogy, a culture of taste: "to educate him," that is, to draw him out of the sphere where the essential has already been missed. Accordingly, philosophy conceived as ethics presupposes not only the abstract polarity of the valid and the non-valid, but a concrete man who has already missed the mark. Such is man as philosophy finds him at the beginning of its route: the man that Parmenides drags along on his journey beyond the gates of Night and Day, the one that Plato draws out of the cave onto the precipitous road of the Sun, the one Descartes rouses from prejudice and leads to truth by way of hyperbolic doubt. Man, such as philosophy takes him at the beginning of its route, is bewildered and lost; he has forgotten the origin.

The enigma thenceforward is the "leap" itself from fallibility to the already fallen. Our anthropological reflection remained short of this leap, but ethics arrives too late. To catch sight of that leap we must make a fresh start and enter upon a new type of reflection bearing on the *avowal* that consciousness makes of it and on the *symbols* of evil in which this avowal is expressed. The hiatus of method between the phenomenology of fallibility and the symbolics of evil only gives expression, therefore, to the hiatus between fallibility and fault in man himself. The symbolics of evil, then, will make a long detour at the end of which it will perhaps be possible to resume the interrupted discourse and reintegrate the findings of that symbolics into a truly *philosophical* anthropology. In this first sense, then, fallibility is *only* the possibility of evil: it indicates the region and the structure of the reality that, through its point of least resistance, offers a "locus" to evil.

But in this first sense the possibility of evil and its actual reality remain external to each other. Now, the very "leap," the very "positing" of evil can in a certain sense be understood starting from the notion of fallibility. Invoking a second sense of the word "possible," we may say that man's disproportion is the possibility of evil: in the sense in which every defection of man remains within the line of his perfection, in which all destitution refers back to man's constitution, in which all degeneration is founded on a "generation into existence"—on a γένεσις εἰς οὐσίαν—to go back to the words of Plato's *Philebus*. Man can invent only human disorders and evils. Thus, because speech is his destination, the evils of idle talk, lying, and flattery are possible. I can imagine the sophist only as a mere semblance of the philosopher; as Plato said, an "image-maker"; and Baal can be only the "idol" of Yahweh. Thus the primordial is the original, the pattern, the paradigm starting from which I can generate all evils, through a kind of *pseudo*-genesis (in the sense in which pathology speaks of disorders as hyper-, as hypo-, or as para-). Man can be evil only in accordance with the lines of force and weakness of his functions and his destination.

No doubt it will be objected, in the style of the Bergsonian critique of the possible, that evil is possible only because it is real and that the concept of fallibility merely records the repercussion of the avowal of the evil that is already in the description of human limitation. That is true: fault carves out behind itself its own possibility and projects it as its shadow onto man's primordial limitation and thus makes it appear fallible. It is undeniable that it is only *through* the currently evil condition of man's heart that one can detect a condition more primordial than any evil: it is through hate and strife that one can perceive the intersubjective structure of the respect that constitutes the difference of consciousnesses; it is through misunderstanding and lying that the primordial structure of speech reveals the identity and otherness of minds. The same holds true for the triple quest of having, power, and worth, perceived through avarice, tyranny, and vainglory. In short, it is always "*through*" the fallen that the primordial shines through. But what does "through" mean? The trans-parency of the primordial through the fallen signifies that avarice, tyranny, and vainglory, first in the order of discovery, of themselves designate having, power, and worth as first in the order of existence. And these "passions," in manifesting the "quests" in which they are rooted, receive from them in return what might be called their mark of downfall. Thus the evil of fault refers intentionally to the primordial; but in return, this reference to the primordial constitutes evil as fault, that is, as di-gression,[8] as de-viation. I can think of evil as evil only "starting from" that from which it falls. The "through" is therefore the correlate of a "starting from"; and it is this "starting from" that allows us to say that fallibility is the *condition* of evil, although evil is the revealer of fallibility.

Can we, then, isolate this representation of the primordial from the description of evil through which the primordial was perceived? Yes, but only in an *imaginary* mode. The imagination of innocence is nothing but the representation of a human life that would realize all its fundamental possibilities without any discrepancy between its primordial destination and its historical manifestation. Innocence would be fallibility without fault, and this fallibility would be only fragility, only weakness, but by no means downfall. It matters little that I can depict innocence only by way of myth, as a state realized

8. *E-cart* [Trans.].

"elsewhere" and "formerly" in localities and in times that have no place in the rational man's geography and history. The essence of the myth of innocence is in giving a symbol of the primordial which shows through in the fallen and which exposes it as fallen. My innocence is my primordial constitution projected in a fanciful history. There is in this imagination nothing scandalous for philosophy. Imagination is an indispensable mode of the investigation of the possible. It might be said, in the style of the Husserlian eidetics, that innocence is the imaginative variation that makes the essence of the primordial constitution stand out, in making it appear *on* another existential modality. At that moment, fallibility is shown as pure possibility without the fallen condition through which it ordinarily appears. Consequently, to say that man is so evil that we no longer know what his goodness would be is really to say nothing at all; for if I do not understand "good," neither do I understand "evil." I need to understand the primordial destination of "goodness" and its historical manifestation in badness together, as a superimpression, so to speak. However primordial badness may be, goodness is yet more primordial. That is why, as we shall see, a myth of fall is possible only within the context of a myth of creation and innocence. If that had been understood, one would not have wondered whether "the image of God" may be lost, as if man stopped being man by becoming bad. Nor would Rousseau have been accused of inconsistency when he obstinately professed man's natural goodness *and* his historical and cultural perversity.

But the concept of fallibility includes the possibility of evil in a still more positive sense: man's disproportion is a *power* to fail, in the sense that it makes man *capable* of failing. As Descartes says: "If I think of myself as participating in nothingness or not-being, in other words, insofar as I am not myself the sovereign Being, I find myself subject to an infinity of imperfections, so that I should not be surprised if I err."[9] *I find myself subject to. . . .* What does this mean? Is it not necessary at the same time to affirm the "leap," the "positing" of evil, the "passage" or "transition" from fallibility to fault?

As we shall see, the myths of fall that most stressed the character of rupture, of the abrupt positing of evil, at the same time relate the subtle sliding, the obscure sag from innocence to evil, as if I could

9. *Meditations* IV.

not depict evil as welling up in the Instant without thinking of it at the same time as intruding and progressing in Duration. It is posited, and it moves ahead. Indeed, beginning from evil as a positing, the contrary aspect of evil as an *Accomplishment of weakness* is uncovered. But this movement of yielding weakness, symbolized in the biblical myth by the figure of Eve, is coextensive with the act by which evil happens. There is something like a dizziness that leads from weakness to temptation and from temptation to fall. Thus evil, in the very moment when "I admit" that I posit it, seems to arise from man's very limitation through the unbroken transition from dizziness. It is this transition from innocence to fault, discovered in the very positing of evil, that gives the concept of fallibility all its equivocal profundity. Fragility is not merely the "locus," the point of insertion of evil, nor even the "origin" starting from which man falls; it is the "capacity" for evil. To say that man is fallible is to say that the limitation peculiar to a being who does not coincide with himself is the primordial weakness from which evil arises. And yet evil *arises* from this weakness only because it is *posited*. This last paradox will be at the center of the symbolics of evil.